The Captain's

PABLO NERUDA

THE CAPTAIN'S VERSES
Los versos del capitán

TRANSLATED BY BRIAN COLE

CΔRCΔNET

Published in Great Britain in 2020 by
Carcanet
Alliance House, 30 Cross Street
Manchester M2 7AQ
www.carcanet.co.uk

A CIP catalogue record for this book is
available from the British Library.

ISBN 978 1 78410 924 0

Printed in Great Britain by SRP Ltd, Exeter, Devon

The publisher acknowledges financial
assistance from Arts Council England.

Contents

Introduction

It is surprising that more of the work of Pablo Neruda has not been translated into English, so that he remains relatively unknown in this country. He is undoubtedly a major figure in the world's literature, as well as dominating twentieth-century South American culture. The award of the Nobel Prize for Literature in 1971 must rank as one of the best deserved in the history of that foundation.

He was born Ricardo Neftalí Reyes Basoalto in 1904 in southern Chile, the son of an engine-driver; only in 1945 did he legally take the name Pablo Neruda. From this humble beginning he built a colourful life as diplomat, communist, senator, freedom fighter, fugitive – but always a poet. His diplomatic duties took him to India and Indonesia, Mexico, Argentina, Spain and France, and he travelled widely in his private capacity in pursuit of his political and literary interests.

In his early life in the Far East he married his first wife, and had a daughter who died young; his journals make little mention of this his only child, or of her mother. Like Sherlock Holmes' 'dog that didn't bark', the absence of comment on his first wife and only child must be evidence of something – was it just that he knew all along that the relationship was a mistake, a young man's folly? Or was the psychic wound too deep for him to express his grief?

In the mid '30s he experienced the Spanish Civil War among Republican sympathisers – including Federico García Lorca, with whom he had become close friends in Argentina. Lorca was murdered by the Fascists in 1936, while Neruda was in Spain. At that time he was also greatly influenced by his second wife, Delia del Carril, and much of his work thereafter is politically committed and idealistic. It was at this time that he became converted to communism. In the aftermath of the collapse of communist societies it is easy to dismiss this conversion as misguided, but we must remember Neruda's experience of Latin American poverty and the excessive gap between the very rich and the very poor, as well as the Spanish Civil War where he lost his close and gifted friend to the extreme right-wing forces. It was natural for him to see the communist ideal as offering the possibility of a better society for his country, and as a way of giving dignity to all its citizens.

Neruda was recalled to Chile in 1938, and then spent three years as Consul-General in Mexico. On his return to Chile in 1943 he formally joined the Communist Party, and was elected to the Senate in 1945. Under the repressive régime of González Videla in Chile, the Party was out-lawed in 1948 and Neruda was forced to flee into exile with Delia, first to Argentina, thence to France. Only in 1954 was he allowed to return to his beloved Chile.

The last fifteen years of his life – apart from a short spell as Ambassador to France – were spent at Isla Negra (his house on the coast near Valparaíso, opposite an island of that name) with his third wife, Matilde Urrutia. His country was ruled by a régime that was more humane than in much of his earlier life, and he no doubt felt he could devote his life to his writing. Indeed, he resigned his ambassadorship after less than two years, because of homesickness for Chile. He had returned for the celebration of his Nobel Prize, and on revisiting Isla Negra decided immediately not to leave it again. He telephoned his resignation to the President, who was then in New York.

In 1973, shortly after the murder of his friend President Salvador Allende and the return of repressive government to Chile, Pablo Neruda died. He had long suffered from cancer of the prostate, and had been ill when the collapse of the Allende régime was announced, but it is very likely that his death was hastened by his sadness at his country's relapse into authoritarianism.

The Captain's Verses celebrates Neruda's love for Matilde Urrutia, his third wife. It was published anonymously in 1952 to spare the feelings of his second wife, Delia, from whom he parted amicably in 1954.

The first section, 'Love', is made up of poems of devotion for his new beloved, and contains some of his most beautiful verses. Some, like 'The Queen', are pure love, and in others ('The Potter', 'Your Feet' i.a.)

Neruda's strong sensuality adds to the force of his loving. In 'Fickle Man' he recognises the philandering side of his nature, and thereby emphasises the depth of his love for Matilde. There is even here in 'Your Laugh' a touch of the poet's consciousness of his mission in life, a very difficult mission, which elsewhere makes him arrogantly demand submission and adoration from his beloved. 'My Son' reads as if written by a father, though Neruda never had a son and had no apparent interest in his one daughter; maybe there is an element here of regretting that he and Matilde are too old to have children.

The last poem in the section, 'Absence', provides a glimpse of the harsh and cruel imagery to come in the first two poems of the next section, 'Desire'. The last poem in this section, 'The Insect', illustrates Neruda's preoccupation with landscapes and geography – and with female bodies. His joy in life and in the senses is an ever-present theme in his work, and some of his most striking similes are between a woman's body and aspects of nature; this theme is further developed, for example, in 'Little America' later in the book. 'The Furies', as its title implies, deals with the darker side of Neruda's love. He is not jealous ('Always'), but arrogant ('The Wrong Step') and demanding: if the beloved is not strong enough to put up with his moods,

> . . . then take
> my sadness and my anger,
> my hostile hands
> which will destroy you a little
> so that you rise up out of the clay,
> made anew for my battles. ('The Hurt')

If she is strong and dedicated to him and his struggle, he promises her everything, but any sign of weakness or less than total devotion brings a threat to leave her as unworthy of him ('Forgetting').

Struggle is the theme of the next section, 'Human Lives', and it is clear that Neruda saw Matilde as an important partner in his political work. In 'The Banner' he writes:

> ... let us go out together
> to fight hand to hand
> against the cobwebs of the wicked,
> against the system that doles out hunger,
> against the organisation of misery.

Despite his apparent need for her, and his welcome of her as a comrade, he makes it clear in 'Dead Woman' that if she died he would carry on the fight '... because you know that I am not only a man but all mankind' – a typical example of Neruda's arrogant conviction of his destiny. 'Not Only Fire' perhaps exemplifies best his determination to be, with Matilde, part of the working class.

The final three sections of the work take up again with passionate intensity Neruda's love of Matilde, of life and of all its sensual experiences. His mission is still present, but without the darker overtones of some of the earlier poems.

I would like to express my gratitude to Charlotte Rundall who helped me enormously at the proofreading stage. Her sensitive and perceptive suggestions were most valuable, and certainly improved the final product.

It is very exciting for a translator to come across a poet of the stature of Neruda who has not been made completely available to the English-speaking world. I have tried to provide a literal translation which would retain the rhythms of the original. While English perhaps lends itself less well to the declamatory style which is so powerful in the Spanish, I hope that Neruda's simple message wrapped up in surprising images will excite the reader, even in translation.

BRIAN COLE

B

Explicación

Mucho se discutió el anonimato de este libro. Lo que yo discutía en mi interior mientras tanto, era si debía o no sacarlo de su origen íntimo: revelar su progenitura era desnudar la intimidad de su nacimiento. Y no me parecía que tal acción fuera leal a los arrebatos de amor y furia, al clima desconsolado y ardiente del destierro que le dio nacimiento.

Por otra parte pienso que todos los libros debieran ser anónimos. Pero entre quitar a todos los míos mi nombre o entregarlo al más misterioso, cedí, por fin, aunque sin muchas ganas.

Que por qué guardó su misterio por tanto tiempo? Por nada y por todo, por lo de aquí y lo de más allá, por alegrías impropias, por sufrimientos ajenos. Cuando Paolo Ricci, compañero luminoso, lo imprimió por primera vez en Nápoles en 1952 pensamos que aquellos escasos ejemplares que él cuidó y preparó con excelencia, desaparecerían sin dejar huellas en las arenas del Sur.

No ha sido así. Y la vida que reclamó su estallido secreto hoy me lo impone como presencia del inconmovible amor.

Entrego, pues, este libro sin explicarlo más, como si fuera mío y no lo fuera: basta con que pudiera andar solo por el mundo y crecer por su cuenta. Ahora que lo reconozco espero que su sangre furiosa me reconocerá también.

PABLO NERUDA

Isla Negra, noviembre 1963

Explanation

There has been much discussion about the anonymity of this book. What I had to discuss with myself however was the question whether or not I should tear it away from its private origin: to reveal its parentage would be to lay bare the privacy of its birth. And it seemed to me that such an act would be a betrayal of the ecstasy of love and rage, of the distressing and passionate atmosphere of exile which gave it birth.

On the other hand I think that all books should be anonymous. However, in considering whether I should withdraw my name from all of mine or give it to the most secret one, I finally gave in, though reluctantly.

But why did it keep its secret for so long? For no reason and for every reason, for obvious and for very recondite ones, for misplaced joy, for the suffering of others. When Paolo Ricci, that radiant companion, printed it in Naples for the first time in 1952 we thought that those few copies that he looked after and produced so splendidly would disappear and leave no trace in the sands of the south.

It was not so. And life that demanded its secret explosion imposes it on me today as the presence of unshakeable love.

So I hand over this book without further explanation, as if it were by me and yet not by me: it is enough that it can make its own way through the world and grow independently. Now that I acknowledge it I hope that its violent blood will also recognise me again.

PABLO NERUDA

Isla Negra, November 1963

Prólogo

de la primera edición anónima de 1952

Haban, 3 de octubre de 1951.

Estimado señor:

Me permito enviarle estos papeles que creo le interesarán y que no he podido dar a la publicidad hasta ahora.

Tengo todos los originales de estos versos. Estan escritos en los sitios más diversos, como trenes, aviones, cafés y en pequeños papelitos extraños en los que no hay casi correcciones. En una de sus últimas cartas venía la *Carta en el Camino*. Muchos de estos papeles por arrugados y cortados son casi ilegibles, pero creo que he logrado descifrarlos.

Mi persona no tiene importancia, pero soy la protagonista de este libro y eso me hace estar orgullosa y satisfecha de mi vida.

Este amor, este gran amor, nació un agosto de un año cualquiera, en mis giras que hacía como artista, por los pueblos de la frontera franco-española.

Él venía de la guerra de España. No venía vencido. Era del partido de Pasionaria, estaba lleno de ilusiones y de esperanzas para su pequeño y lejano país, en Centro América.

Siento no poder dar su nombre. Nunca he sabido cuál era el verdadero, si Martínez, Ramírez, o Sánchez. Yo lo llamo simplemente mi Capitán y éste es el nombre que quiero conservar en este libro.

Sus versos son como él mismo: tiernos, amorosos, apasionados, y terribles en su cólera. Era fuerte y su fuerza la sentían todos los que a él se acercaban. Era un hombre privilegiado de los que nacen para grandes destinos. Yo sentía su fuerza y mi placer más grande era sentirme pequeña a su lado.

Entró a mi vida, como él lo dice en un verso, echando la puerta abajo. No golpeó la puerta con timidez de enamorado. Desde el primer instante, él se sintió dueño de mi cuerpo y de mi alma. Me hizo sentir que todo cambiaba en mi vida, esa pequeña vida mía de artista, de comodidad, de blandura, se transformó como todo lo que él tocaba.

Preface

to the first, anonymous edition of 1952

Havana, 3rd October 1951

Dear Sir,

I take the liberty of sending you these papers which I believe will interest you and which until now I have not been able to make public.

I possess all the originals of these verses. They were written in a wide variety of places, in trains, aeroplanes, cafés, on strange scraps of paper, almost without corrections. In one of his last letters came the 'Letter on my Travels'. Many of these papers are almost illegible because they are crumpled and torn, but I believe I have succeeded in deciphering them.

I myself am not important, but I am the protagonist of this book and that makes me proud and satisfied with my life.

This love, this great love, began one year in August, on one of the tours that I made as an artist through the towns and villages on the Franco-Spanish border.

He came from the war in Spain. He did not come as one of the defeated. He belonged to the party of La Pasionaria, he was full of illusions and hopes for his small and distant land in Central America.

Unfortunately I cannot tell you his name. I never found out which was the true one, Martínez, Ramírez or Sánchez. I just call him my Captain, and that is the name that I would like to keep in this book.

His verses are like himself: tender, loving, passionate and terrible in anger. He was strong, and everyone who came near him felt his strength. He was a privileged man, one of those born for a great destiny. I felt his strength, and my greatest pleasure was to feel small at his side.

He came into my life, as he says in one of the verses 'breaking down the door'. He did not knock on the door with the shyness of a lover. From the first moment he felt himself lord of my body and my soul. He made me feel that he was changing everything in my life; my little artist's life of comfort and softness was transformed like everything else that he touched.

15

No sabía de sentimientos pequeños, ni tampoco los aceptaba. Me dio su amor, con toda la pasión que él era capaz de sentir y yo lo amé como nunca me creí capaz de amar. Todo se transformó en mi vida. Entré a un mundo que antes nunca soñé que existía. Primero tuve miedo, hubo momentos de duda, pero el amor no me dejó vacilar mucho tiempo.

Este amor me traía todo. La ternura dulce y sencilla cuando buscaba una flor, un juguete, una piedra de río y me la entregaba con sus ojos húmedos de una ternura infinita. Sus grandes manos eran en este momento, de una blandura dulce y en sus ojos se asomaba entonces un alma de niño.

Pero había en mí un pasado que él no conocía y había celos y furias incontenibles. Éstas eran como tempestades furiosas que azotaban su alma y la mía, pero nunca tuvieron fuerza para destrozar la cadena que nos unía, que era nuestro amor, y de cada tempestad salíamos más unidos, más fuertes, más seguros de nosotros mismos.

En todos estos momentos, él escribía estos versos, que me hacían subir al cielo o bajar al mismo infierno, con la crudeza de sus palabras que me quemaban como brasas.

Él no podía amar de otra manera. Estos versos son la historia de nuestro amor, grande en todas sus manifestaciones. Tenía la misma pasión que él ponía en sus combates, en sus luchas contra las injusticias. Le dolía el sufrimiento y la miseria, no sólo de su pueblo, sino de todos los pueblos, todas las luchas por combatirlas eran suyas y se entregaba entero, con toda su pasión.

Yo soy muy poco literaria y no puedo hablar del valor de estos versos, fuera del valor humano que indiscutiblemente tienen. Tal vez el Capitán nunca pensó que estos versos se publicarían, pero ahora creo que es mi deber darlos al mundo.

Saluda atentamente a Ud.

ROSARIO DE LA CERDA

He knew no small feelings, and accepted none either. He gave me his love with all the passion that he was capable of feeling, and I loved him as I never thought myself capable of loving. Everything in my life was transformed. I entered a world whose existence I had never previously dreamt of. At first I was afraid, I had moments of doubt, but love did not let me hesitate long.

This love gave me everything. The gentle, simple tenderness when he picked out a flower, a toy, a river pebble and handed it to me, his eyes moist with infinite tenderness. His large hands were at this moment soft and gentle, and in his eyes could be seen the soul of a child.

But there was in me a past which he did not know, and there were attacks of jealousy and uncontainable rage. They were like furious thunderstorms which lashed his soul and mine, but they never had the strength to break the chain that linked us, that was our love, and we came out of every storm closer, stronger, more sure of ourselves.

In all these moments he wrote these verses which raised me up to Heaven or cast me down to the depths of Hell itself with the roughness of his words which burned me like glowing coals.

He could not love in any other way. These verses are the history of our love, great in all its manifestations. It had the same passion with which he applied himself to his battles, his struggles against injustices. He suffered from the pain and misery not only of his people, but of all peoples; all battles waged against them were his battles, and he committed himself with his whole being, with all his passion.

I am not very literary and cannot speak about the value of these verses, apart from the human value they indisputably have. Perhaps the Captain never thought that these verses would be published, but now I believe it is my duty to bring them to the light of the world.

Yours faithfully,

ROSARIO DE LA CERDA

Love

El amor

En ti la tierra

Pequeña
rosa,
rosa pequeña,
a veces,
diminuta y desnuda,
parece
que en una mano mía
cabes,
que así voy a cerrarte
y a llevarte a mi boca,
pero
de pronto
mis pies tocan tus pies y mi boca tus labios,
has crecido,
suben tus hombros como dos colinas,
tus pechos se pasean por mi pecho,
mi brazo alcanza apenas a rodear la delgada
línea de luna nueva que tiene tu cintura:
en el amor como agua de mar te has desatado:
mido apenas los ojos más extensos del cielo
y me inclino a tu boca para besar la tierra.

In You the Earth

Little
rose,
rose so little,
tiny and naked,
sometimes
it seems
that you would fit into just one
of my hands,
and that so I could close you in
and raise you to my mouth,
but
suddenly
my feet touch your feet and my mouth your lips,
you have grown,
your shoulders rise up like two hills,
your breasts make their way across my breast,
my arm can scarcely encircle the slender
new-moon line that is your waist;
like surging waves you have broken out in love;
I can hardly measure the widest eyes of the heavens
and I bend down to your mouth to kiss the earth.

La reina

Yo te he nombrado reina.
Hay más altas que tú, más altas.
Hay más puras que tú, más puras.
Hay más bellas que tú, hay más bellas.

Pero tú eres la reina.

Cuando vas por las calles
nadie te reconoce.
Nadie ve tu corona de cristal, nadie mira
la alfombra de oro rojo
que pisas donde pasas,
la alfombra que no existe.

Y cuando asomas
suenan todos los ríos
en mi cuerpo, sacuden
el cielo las campanas,
y un himno llena el mundo.

Sólo tú y yo,
sólo tú y yo, amor mío,
lo escuchamos.

The Queen

I have appointed you queen.
There are greater women than you, greater.
There are purer women than you, purer.
There are more beautiful women than you, there are.

But you are the queen.

When you walk through the streets
no one recognises you.
No one sees your crystal crown, no one notices
the carpet of red gold
which you tread as you pass,
the carpet that does not exist.

And when you appear
all the rivers roar
in my body, bells
shake the heavens,
and the world is filled with a hymn.

Only you and I,
only you and I, my love,
only we hear it.

El alfarero

Todo tu cuerpo tiene
copa o dulzura destinada a mí.

Cuando subo la mano
encuentro en cada sitio una paloma
que me buscaba, como
si te hubieran, amor, hecho de arcilla
para mis propias manos de alfarero.

Tus rodillas, tus senos,
tu cintura
faltan en mí como en el hueco
de una tierra sedienta
de la que desprendieron
una forma,
y juntos
somos completos como un solo río,
como una sola arena.

The Potter

Your whole body possesses
a cup or sweetness destined for me.

When I lift my hand
I find in each place a dove
which was seeking me, as if they had
made you, my love, out of clay
for my own potter's hands.

Your knees, your breasts,
your waist,
I feel their loss like the hollow space
in a thirsting earth
from which they had taken away
this form,
and together
we are complete like a single river,
like a single beach.

8 de septiembre

Hoy, este día fue una copa plena,
hoy, este día fue la inmensa ola,
hoy, fue toda la tierra.

Hoy el mar tempestuoso
nos levantó en un beso
tan alto que temblamos
a la luz de un relámpago
y, atados, descendimos
a sumergirnos sin desenlazarnos.

Hoy nuestros cuerpos se hicieron extensos,
crecieron hasta el límite del mundo
y rodaron fundiéndose
en una sola gota
de cera o meteoro.

Entre tú y yo se abrió una nueva puerta
y alguien, sin rostro aún,
allí nos esperaba.

The 8th of September

Today, this day was a full glass,
today, this day was a towering wave,
today was the whole earth.

Today the tempestuous sea
lifted us up in a kiss
so high that we trembled
in the glare of lightning
and, bound together, we came down
and both went under, still entwined.

Today our bodies stretched out,
grew to the edges of the world
and rolled on, fusing
into a single drop
of wax, a single meteor.

Between you and me a new door opened
and someone, as yet faceless,
was waiting for us there.

Tus pies

Cuando no puedo mirar tu cara
miro tus pies.

Tus pies de hueso arqueado,
tus pequeños pies duros.

Yo sé que te sostienen,
y que tu dulce peso
sobre ellos se levanta.

Tu cintura y tus pechos,
la duplicada púrpura
de tus pezones,
la caja de tus ojos
que recién han volado,
tu ancha boca de fruta,
tu cabellera roja,
pequeña torre mía.

Pero no amo tus pies
sino porque anduvieron
sobre la tierra y sobre
el viento y sobre el agua,
hasta que me encontraron.

Your Feet

When I cannot gaze on your face
I gaze on your feet.

Your feet of arched bone,
your small, hard feet.

I know they hold you up,
and that your sweet weight
rises up upon them.

Your waist and your breasts,
the double purple
of your nipples,
the casing of your eyes
which have just flown away,
your wide fruit-mouth,
your red hair,
my little tower.

But I only love your feet
because they have wandered
over the earth and through
the wind and over the water,
until they brought you to me.

Tus manos

Cuando tus manos salen,
amor, hacia las mías,
qué me traen volando?
Por qué se detuvieron
en mi boca, de pronto,
por qué las reconozco
como si entonces, antes,
las hubiera tocado,
como si antes de ser
hubieran recorrido
mi frente, mi cintura?

Su suavidad venía
volando sobre el tiempo,
sobre el mar, sobre el humo,
sobre la primavera,
y cuando tú pusiste
tus manos en mi pecho,
reconocí esas alas
de paloma dorada,
reconocí esa greda
y ese color de trigo.

Los años de mi vida
yo caminé buscándolas.
Subí las escaleras,
crucé los arrecifes,
me llevaron los trenes,
las aguas me trajeron,

Your Hands

When your hands, my love,
move out towards mine,
what do they bring me in their flight?
Why did they stop
on my mouth, suddenly,
why do I recognise them
as if long ago, before,
I had touched them,
as if before they existed
they had already stroked
my brow and my waist?

Their softness came
flying through time,
over the sea, through the smoke,
with the spring,
and when you placed
your hands on my breast
I knew those wings
of golden doves,
I knew that clay
and that colour of wheat.

All the years of my life
I have been in search of them.
I climbed up flights of stairs,
I sailed through jagged reefs,
trains carried me off,
the waters brought me back,

y en la piel de las uvas
me pareció tocarte.
La madera de pronto
me trajo tu contacto,
la almendra me anunciaba
tu suavidad secreta,
hasta que se cerraron
tus manos en mi pecho
y allí como dos alas
terminaron su viaje.

and on the skin of grapes
I thought I touched you.
The feel of wood suddenly
brought me in contact with you,
the almond gave me promise
of your secret softness,
until your two hands
closed over my breast
and there like two wings
completed their voyage.

Tu risa

Quítame el pan, si quieres,
quítame el aire, pero
no me quites tu risa.

No me quites la rosa,
la lanza que desgranas,
el agua que de pronto
estalla en tu alegría,
la repentina ola
de planta que te nace.

Mi lucha es dura y vuelvo
con los ojos cansados
a veces de haber visto
la tierra que no cambia,
pero al entrar tu risa
sube al cielo buscándome
y abre para mí todas
las puertas de la vida.

Amor mío, en la hora
más oscura desgrana
tu risa, y si de pronto
ves que mi sangre mancha
las piedras de la calle,
ríe, porque tu risa
será para mis manos
como una espada fresca.

Your Laugh

Take away my bread, if you will,
take away the air, but
do not take away your laugh.

Do not take away the rose,
the spear which you unsheathe,
the water that all at once
bursts up in your joy,
the sudden wave of plants
that springs up at your feet.

My struggle is hard and sometimes
I come home tired-eyed
from having gazed all day
at the unchanging earth,
but as soon as I come in, your laugh
rises to heaven, seeking me out,
and opens up for me
all the doors of life.

My love, even in the hour
of deepest darkness unsheathe
your laugh, and if suddenly
you see my blood staining
the stones in the street,
then laugh, because your laugh
will be for my hands
like a fresh gleaming sword.

Junto al mar en otoño,
tu risa debe alzar
su cascada de espuma,
y en primavera, amor,
quiero tu risa como
la flor que yo esperaba,
la flor azul, la rosa
de mi patria sonora.

Ríete de la noche,
del día, de la luna,
ríete de las calles
torcidas de la isla,
ríete de este torpe
muchacho que te quiere,
pero cuando yo abro
los ojos y los cierro,
cuando mis pasos van,
cuando vuelven mis pasos,
niégame el pan, el aire,
la luz, la primavera,
pero tu risa nunca
porque me moriría.

By the sea in autumn
your laugh should spout up
its shower of foam,
and in spring, my love,
I need your laugh
like the long-awaited flower,
the blue flower, the rose
of my melodious homeland.

Laugh at the night,
at the day, at the moon,
laugh at the crookedness
of streets on our island,
laugh at this awkward
boy who loves you,
but when I open
my eyes and close them,
when my footsteps pace on,
and when my footsteps return,
deny me bread, and air,
deny me light, and spring,
but never your laugh,
for I should surely die.

El inconstante

Los ojos se me fueron
tras una morena que pasó.

Era de nácar negro,
era de uvas moradas,
y me azotó la sangre
con su cola de fuego.

Detrás de todas
me voy.

Pasó una clara rubia
como una planta de oro
balanceando sus dones.
Y mi boca se fue
como con una ola
descargando en su pecho
relámpagos de sangre.

Detrás de todas
me voy.

Pero a ti, sin moverme,
sin verte, tú distante,
van mi sangre y mis besos,
morena y clara mía,
alta y pequeña mía,
ancha y delgada mía,
mi fea, mi hermosura,

Fickle Man

My eyes ran away with me
after a dark woman passing by.

She was black mother-of-pearl,
she was dark violet grapes,
and my blood lashed me
with its fiery tail.

I chase after
them all.

A bright blonde went by
like a golden plant
swinging the gifts of her body.
And my mouth ran away with me
as with a wave of the sea
unloading on her breast
lightning flashes of blood.

I chase after
them all.

But to you, without my moving,
without seeing you, in the distance,
to you go out my blood and kisses,
my dark and blonde woman,
my lofty and small woman,
my robust and slender woman,
my ugly one, my beauty,

hecha de todo el oro
y de toda la plata,
hecha de todo el trigo
y de toda la tierra,
hecha de toda el agua
de las olas marinas,
hecha para mis brazos,
hecha para mis besos,
hecha para mi alma.

made of all the gold and all
the silver in the world,
made of all the wheat
and of all the earth,
made of all the water
of the waves of the sea,
made for my arms,
made for my kisses,
made for my soul.

La noche en la isla

Toda la noche he dormido contigo
junto al mar, en la isla.
Salvaje y dulce eras entre el placer y el sueño,
entre el fuego y el agua.

Tal vez muy tarde
nuestros sueños se unieron
en lo alto o en el fondo,
arriba como ramas que un mismo viento mueve,
abajo como rojas raíces que se tocan.

Tal vez tu sueño
se separó del mío
y por el mar oscuro
me buscaba
como antes
cuando aún no existías,
cuando sin divisarte
navegué por tu lado,
y tus ojos buscaban
lo que ahora
— pan, vino, amor y cólera —
te doy a manos llenas
porque tú eres la copa
que esperaba los dones de mi vida.

He dormido contigo
toda la noche mientras
la oscura tierra gira

Night on the Island

The whole night long I have slept with you
next to the sea, on the island.
You were wild and gentle between pleasure and dreams,
between fire and water.

Perhaps very late
our dreams were united
in the heights or in the depths,
on high like branches moved by the same wind,
down below like red roots touching each other.

Perhaps your dream
broke away from mine
and searched for me
across the darkness of the sea
as before
when you did not yet exist,
when without noticing you
I sailed right past you,
and your eyes searched for
those things which now
– bread, wine, love and anger –
I give you by the handful
because you are the goblet
that was waiting for the gifts of my life.

I have slept with you
the whole night long,
while the dark earth turns

con vivos y con muertos,
y al despertar de pronto
en medio de la sombra
mi brazo rodeaba tu cintura.
Ni la noche, ni el sueño
pudieron separarnos.

He dormido contigo
y al despertar tu boca
salida de tu sueño
me dio el sabor de tierra,
de agua marina, de algas,
del fondo de tu vida,
y recibí tu beso
mojado por la aurora
como si me llegara
del mar que nos rodea.

with the living and the dead,
and when I awoke suddenly
in the middle of the darkness
my arm was round your waist.
Neither night nor our dreams
could separate us.

I have slept with you
and when I awoke your mouth
coming out of your dream
gave me the taste of the earth,
of sea-water, of seaweed,
from the depths of your life,
and I received your kiss
moistened by the dawn
as if it came to me
from the sea which encircles us.

El viento en la isla

El viento es un caballo:
óyelo cómo corre
por el mar, por el cielo.

Quiere llevarme: escucha
cómo recorre el mundo
para llevarme lejos.

Escóndeme en tus brazos
por esta noche sola,
mientras la lluvia rompe
contra el mar y la tierra
su boca innumerable.

Escucha cómo el viento
me llama galopando
para llevarme lejos.

Con tu frente en mi frente,
con tu boca en mi boca,
atados nuestros cuerpos
al amor que nos quema,
deja que el viento pase
sin que pueda llevarme.

Deja que el viento corra
coronado de espuma,
que me llame y me busque
galopando en la sombra,

The Wind on the Island

The wind is a horse;
hear how he runs
over the sea, through the sky.

He wants to carry me off; listen
how he scours the earth
to carry me off to distant lands.

Hide me in your arms
just for this one night,
while the rain bursts
against the sea and the land
from its innumerable mouth.

Listen how the wind
calls me as he gallops
to carry me off to distant lands.

With your brow pressed to my brow,
with your mouth pressed to my mouth,
our two bodies bound
to the love that scorches us,
let the wind pass on
without taking me with him.

Let the wind run on
crowned with spray from the sea,
let him call me and search for me
galloping through the darkness,

mientras yo, sumergido
bajo tus grandes ojos,
por esta noche sola
descansaré, amor mío.

while I, submerged
in your wide, deep eyes
just for this one night
have my fill of sleep, my love.

La infinita

Ves estas manos? Han medido
la tierra, han separado
los minerales y los cereales,
han hecho la paz y la guerra,
han derribado las distancias
de todos los mares y ríos,
y sin embargo
cuando te recorren
a ti, pequeña,
grano de trigo, alondra,
no alcanzan a abarcarte,
se cansan alcanzando
las palomas gemelas
que reposan o vuelan en tu pecho,
recorren las distancias de tus piernas,
se enrollan en la luz de tu cintura.
Para mí eres tesoro más cargado
de inmensidad que el mar y sus racimos
y eres blanca y azul y extensa como
la tierra en la vendimia.
En ese territorio,
de tus pies a tu frente,
andando, andando, andando,
me pasaré la vida.

My Infinity

Do you see these hands? They have measured
the earth, have separated
minerals and cereals,
they have made peace and war,
they have conquered the distances
of all seas and rivers,
but nevertheless
when they travel over
you, my little one,
my grain of wheat, my lark,
they cannot encompass you,
they tire when they try to reach
the twin doves
that rest or fly on your breast,
they traverse the length of your legs,
they coil up in the light of your waist.
For me you are a treasure of value
more immense than the sea and its fruits
and you are white and blue and broad like
the earth when grapes are ripe.
In this territory,
between your feet and your brow,
strolling, strolling, strolling,
I shall spend my life.

Bella

Bella,
como en la piedra fresca
del manantial, el agua
abre un ancho relámpago de espuma,
así es la sonrisa en tu rostro,
bella.

Bella,
de finas manos y delgados pies
como un caballito de plata,
andando, flor del mundo,
así te veo,
bella.

Bella,
con un nido de cobre enmarañado
en tu cabeza, un nido
color de miel sombría
donde mi corazón arde y reposa,
bella.

Bella,
no te caben los ojos en la cara,
no te caben los ojos en la tierra.
Hay países, hay ríos,
en tus ojos,
mi patria está en tus ojos,
yo camino por ellos,
ellos dan luz al mundo

Beauty

Beauty,
as in the cool stone
of the spring the water
launches a broad sheet of foam-lightning,
so is the smile in your eyes,
my beauty.

Beauty,
with fine hands and delicate feet
like a little silver horse,
high-stepping, flower of the world,
so I see you,
my beauty.

Beauty,
with a nest of copper entangled
in your hair, a nest
the colour of dark honey
where my heart burns and finds rest,
my beauty.

Beauty,
your face cannot contain your eyes,
the earth cannot contain your eyes.
There are countries, there are rivers
in your eyes,
my homeland is in your eyes,
I walk through them,
they give light to the world

por donde yo camino,
bella.

Bella,
tus senos son como dos panes hechos
de tierra cereal y luna de oro,
bella.

Bella,
tu cintura
la hizo mi brazo como un río cuando
pasó mil años por tu dulce cuerpo,
bella.

Bella,
no hay nada como tus caderas,
tal vez la tierra tiene
en algún sitio oculto
la curva y el aroma de tu cuerpo,
tal vez en algún sitio,
bella.

Bella, mi bella,
tu voz, tu piel, tus uñas,
bella, mi bella,
tu ser, tu luz, tu sombra,
bella,
todo eso es mío, bella,
todo eso es mío, mía,
cuando andas o reposas,
cuando cantas o duermes,
cuando sufres o sueñas,

through which I walk,
my beauty.

Beauty,
your breasts are like two loaves made
of cereal earth and golden moon,
my beauty.

Beauty,
your waist
was formed by my arm like a river flowing
for a thousand years over your sweet body,
my beauty.

Beauty,
there is nothing like your hips,
perhaps the earth offers
in some hidden place
the curve and fragrance of your body,
perhaps in some place,
my beauty.

Beauty, my beauty,
your voice, your skin, your nails,
beauty, my beauty,
your being, your light, your shade,
beauty,
all this is mine, beauty,
all this is mine, my beauty,
when you walk or rest,
when you sing or sleep,
when you suffer or dream,

siempre,
cuando estás cerca o lejos,
siempre,
eres mía, mi bella,
siempre.

always,
when you are near or far away,
always,
you are mine, my beauty,
always.

La rama robada

En la noche entraremos
a robar
una rama florida.

Pasaremos el muro,
en las tinieblas del jardín ajeno,
dos sombras en la sombra.

Aún no se fue el invierno,
y el manzano aparece
convertido de pronto
en cascada de estrellas olorosas.

En la noche entraremos
hasta su tembloroso firmamento,
y tus pequeñas manos y las mías
robarán las estrellas.

Y sigilosamente,
a nuestra casa,
en la noche y la sombra,
entrará con tus pasos
el silencioso paso del perfume
y con pies estrellados
el cuerpo claro de la Primavera.

The Stolen Branch

We shall go into the night
to steal
a flowering branch.

We shall climb over the wall,
in the darkness of someone's garden,
two shadows in the shadow.

Winter is still not past
and the apple tree appears
suddenly transformed into
a cascade of perfumed stars.

We shall go into the night
right up to its trembling firmament,
and your little hands and mine
will steal the stars.

And then secretly,
in our home,
in the night and the dark,
there will enter with your steps
the silent tread of the perfume,
and with starry feet
the shining body of Spring.

El hijo

Ay hijo, sabes, sabes
de dónde vienes?

De un lago con gaviotas
blancas y hambrientas.

Junto al agua de invierno
ella y yo levantamos
una fogata roja
gastándonos los labios
de besarnos el alma,
echando al fuego todo,
quemándonos la vida.

Así llegaste al mundo.

Pero ella para verme
y para verte un día
atravesó los mares
y yo para abrazar
su pequeña cintura
toda la tierra anduve,
con guerras y montañas,
con arenas y espinas.

Así llegaste al mundo.

De tantos sitios vienes,
del agua y de la tierra,

My Son

My son, do you know, do you know
where you come from?

From a lake with seagulls
crying, white and hungry.

By the wintry waters
she and I built up
a red blazing fire
wearing away our lips
with kisses to our souls,
throwing everything into the flames,
and scorching our lives.

That is how you came into the world.

But she, to see me
and to see you one day
crossed over the oceans,
and I, to embrace
her tiny waist,
travelled all the earth,
with its wars and mountains,
with its deserts and thorns.

That is how you came into the world.

You come from so many places,
from the water and the earth,

del fuego y de la nieve,
de tan lejos caminas
hacia nosotros dos,
desde el amor terrible
que nos ha encadenado,
que queremos saber
cómo eres, qué nos dices,
porque tú sabes más
del mundo que te dimos.

Como una gran tormenta
sacudimos nosotros
el árbol de la vida
hasta las más ocultas
fibras de las raíces
y apareces ahora
cantando en el follaje,
en la más alta rama
que contigo alcanzamos.

from the fire and the snow,
you come from so far
to be with us two,
from this terrible love
which holds us in chains,
that we want to know
what you are, what you can tell us,
because you know more
of the world which we gave you.

Like a great tempest
we shook and shook
the tree of life
down to the most secret
fibres of its roots,
and now you appear
singing in the leaves,
on the highest branch
that we reached with you.

La tierra

La tierra verde se ha entregado
a todo lo amarillo, oro, cosechas,
terrones, hojas, grano,
pero cuando el otoño se levanta
con su estandarte extenso
eres tú la que veo,
es para mí tu cabellera
la que reparte las espigas.

Veo los monumentos
de antigua piedra rota,
pero si toco
la cicatriz de piedra
tu cuerpo me responde,
mis dedos reconocen
de pronto, estremecidos,
tu caliente dulzura.

Entre los héroes paso
recién condecorados
por la tierra y la pólvora
y detrás de ellos, muda,
con tus pequeños pasos,
eres o no eres?

Ayer, cuando sacaron
de raíz, para verlo,
el viejo árbol enano,
te vi salir mirándome

The Earth

The green earth has yielded
to all the yellow, gold, the harvests,
lumps of soil, leaves, the corn,
but when autumn rises up
with its broad banner
you are the one that I see,
for me it is your hair
that brings to us the ears of corn.

I see the monuments
of ancient, broken stone,
but if I touch
the scar of stone,
your body gives me answer,
my fingers recognise
with sudden thrill
the warmth of your sweetness.

I pass among the heroes,
those newly decorated
by the earth and the dust,
and behind them, mute,
with your small steps,
is it you or is it not you?

Yesterday, when they pulled out
the old stunted tree
by the roots, just to see,
I saw you looking out at me

desde las torturadas
y sedientas raíces.

Y cuando viene el sueño
a extenderme y llevarme
a mi propio silencio
hay un gran viento blanco
que derriba mi sueño
y caen de él las hojas,
caen como cuchillos
sobre mí desangrándome.

Y cada herida tiene
la forma de tu boca.

from the tortured
and thirsting roots.

And when sleep comes
to stretch me out and take me off
to my own silence
there is a great white wind
which overthrows my sleep,
and the leaves fall from it,
fall like knives
on me and draw my blood.

And every wound bears
the shape of your mouth.

Ausencia

Apenas te he dejado,
vas en mí, cristalina
o temblorosa,
o inquieta, herida por mí mismo
o colmada de amor, como cuando tus ojos
se cierran sobre el don de la vida
que sin cesar te entrego.

Amor mío,
nos hemos encontrado
sedientos y nos hemos
bebido toda el agua y la sangre,
nos encontramos
con hambre
y nos mordimos
como el fuego muerde,
dejándonos heridas.

Pero espérame,
guárdame tu dulzura.
Yo te daré también
una rosa.

Absence

Scarcely have I left you
than you are with me, crystalline
or trembling,
or anxious, wounded by myself,
or overflowing with love, as when your eyes
close upon the gift of life
which ceaselessly I give you.

My love,
we found each other
thirsting, and we drank up
all the water and the blood,
we met each other
hungering,
and we bit each other
as the fire bites,
leaving bleeding wounds.

But wait for me,
preserve for me your sweetness.
I shall also give you
a rose.

Desire

El deseo

El tigre

Soy el tigre.
Te acecho entre las hojas
anchas como lingotes
de mineral mojado.

El río blanco crece
bajo la niebla. Llegas.

Desnuda te sumerges.
Espero.

Entonces en un salto
de fuego, sangre, dientes,
de un zarpazo derribo
tu pecho, tus caderas.

Bebo tu sangre, rompo
tus miembros uno a uno.

Y me quedo velando
por años en la selva
tus huesos, tu ceniza,
inmóvil, lejos
del odio y de la cólera,
desarmado en tu muerte,
cruzado por las lianas,
inmóvil en la lluvia,
centinela implacable
de mi amor asesino.

The Tiger

I am the tiger.
I stalk you among leaves
as broad as streaming
ingots of metal.

The white river swells
beneath the mist. You are coming.

Naked you dive under.
I wait.

Then with one leap
of fire, blood, teeth,
I claw down to the earth
your breast, your hips.

I drink your blood, I break
your limbs one by one.

And I stay on guard
for years in the jungle
over your bones, your ashes,
motionless, far removed
from hate and anger,
disarmed by your death,
enlaced by lianas,
motionless in the rain
an implacable sentinel
in my murderous love.

El cóndor

Yo soy el cóndor, vuelo
sobre ti que caminas
y de pronto en un ruedo
de viento, pluma, garras,
te asalto y te levanto
en un ciclón silbante
de huracanado frío.

Y a mi torre de nieve,
a mi guarida negra
te llevo y sola vives,
y te llenas de plumas
y vuelas sobre el mundo,
inmóvil, en la altura.

Hembra cóndor, saltemos
sobre esta presa roja,
desgarremos la vida
que pasa palpitando
y levantemos juntos
nuestro vuelo salvaje.

The Condor

I am the condor, I circle
above you as you walk
and suddenly in a swirl
of wind, feathers, talons,
I fall on you and carry you up
in a shrill cyclone
of stormy cold.

Up to my snowy tower
to my black lair
I carry you off to live alone,
you grow a covering of feathers
and you fly over the world,
motionless, in the heights.

Condor wife, let us plunge
on this red prey,
let us tear out the life
that comes along with beating heart
and let us rise again together
into our wild flight.

El insecto

De tus caderas a tus pies
quiero hacer un largo viaje.

Soy más pequeño que un insecto.

Voy por estas colinas,
son de color de avena,
tienen delgadas huellas
que sólo yo conozco,
centímetros quemados,
pálidas perspectivas.

Aquí hay una montaña.
No saldré nunca de ella.
Oh qué musgo gigante!
Y un cráter, una rosa
de fuego humedecido!

Por tus piernas desciendo
hilando una espiral
o durmiendo en el viaje
y llego a tus rodillas
de redonda dureza
como a las cimas duras
de un claro continente.

Hacia tus pies resbalo,
a las ocho aberturas
de tus dedos agudos,

The Insect

From your hips down to your feet
I want to make a long journey.

I am smaller than an insect.

Over these hills I pass,
hills the colour of oats,
crossed with faint tracks
that only I know,
scorched centimetres,
pale perspectives.

Now here is a mountain.
I shall never leave this.
What a giant growth of moss!
And a crater, a rose
of moist fire!

Coming down your legs
I trace a spiral,
or sleep on the way,
and arrive at your knees,
round hardness
like the hard peaks
of a bright continent.

Sliding down to your feet
I reach the eight slits
of your pointed, slow,

lentos, peninsulares,
y de ellos al vacío
de la sábana blanca
caigo, buscando ciego
y hambriento tu contorno
de vasija quemante!

peninsular toes,
and from them I fall down
to the white emptiness
of the sheet, seeking blindly
and hungrily the form
of your fiery crucible!

The Furies

Las furias

El amor

Qué tienes, qué tenemos,
qué nos pasa?
Ay nuestro amor es una cuerda dura
que nos amarra hiriéndonos
y si queremos
salir de nuestra herida,
separarnos,
nos hace un nuevo nudo y nos condena
a desangrarnos y quemarnos juntos.

Qué tienes? Yo te miro
y no hallo nada en ti sino dos ojos
como todos los ojos, una boca
perdida entre mil bocas que besé, más hermosas,
un cuerpo igual a los que resbalaron
bajo mi cuerpo sin dejar memoria.

Y qué vacía por el mundo ibas
como una jarra de color de trigo
sin aire, sin sonido, sin substancia!
Yo busqué en vano en ti
profundidad para mis brazos
que excavan, sin cesar, bajo la tierra:
bajo tu piel, bajo tus ojos
nada,
bajo tu doble pecho levantado
apenas
una corriente de orden cristalino
que no sabe por qué corre cantando.
Por qué, por qué, por qué,
amor mío, por qué?

Love

What is the matter with you? With us?
What is happening to us?
Ah, our love is a harsh cord
which ties us fast and sears
and if ever we wish
to escape our wounds,
to separate,
it makes a new knot for us and condemns us
to bleed and burn together.

What is the matter with you? I look at you
and I find nothing in you but two eyes
just like any eyes, a mouth
lost among a thousand more beautiful mouths I have kissed,
a body just like those that slid
beneath my body and left no memory.

And how empty you walked through the world
like a pitcher the colour of wheat
without air, without sound, without substance!
In vain I sought in you
depth for my arms
which dig ceaselessly under the earth;
under your skin, behind your eyes,
nothing,
under the double swell of your breasts
scarcely
a flow of crystal liquid
that does not know why it flows and sings.
Why, why, why,
my love, why?

Siempre

Antes de mí
no tengo celos.

Ven con un hombre
a la espalda,
ven con cien hombres en tu cabellera,
ven con mil hombres entre tu pecho y tus pies,
ven como un río
lleno de ahogados
que encuentra el mar furioso,
la espuma eterna, el tiempo!

Tráelos todos
adonde yo te espero:
siempre estaremos solos,
siempre estaremos tú y yo
solos sobre la tierra,
para comenzar la vida!

Always

I am not jealous
of what came before me.

Come with a man
on your shoulders,
come with a hundred men in your hair,
come with a thousand men between your breasts and your feet,
come like a river
full of drowned men
which flows down to the wild sea,
to the eternal surf, to Time!

Bring them all
to where I am waiting for you;
we shall always be alone,
we shall always be you and I
alone on earth,
to start our life!

El desvío

Si tu pie se desvía de nuevo,
será cortado.

Si tu mano te lleva
a otro camino
se caerá podrida.

Si me apartas tu vida
morirás
aunque vivas.

Seguirás muerta o sombra,
andando sin mí por la tierra.

The Wrong Step

If your foot takes another wrong step
it will be severed.

If your hand brings you
to another road
it will rot and fall off.

If you take away your life from me
you will die
even while you live.

You will be a corpse or shadow,
wandering through the world without me.

La pregunta

Amor, una pregunta
te ha destrozado.

Yo he regresado a ti
desde la incertidumbre con espinas.

Te quiero recta como
la espada o el camino.

Pero te empeñas
en guardar un recodo
de sombra que no quiero.

Amor mío,
compréndeme,
te quiero toda,
de ojos a pies, a uñas,
por dentro,
toda la claridad, la que guardabas.

Soy yo, amor mío,
quien golpea tu puerta.
No es el fantasma, no es
el que antes se detuvo
en tu ventana.
Yo echo la puerta abajo:
yo entro en toda tu vida:
vengo a vivir en tu alma:
tú no puedes conmigo.

The Question

My love, one question
has destroyed you.

I have come back to you
from thorn-filled uncertainty.

I want you as straight
as a sword or the road.

But you insist
on keeping a loop
of shadow that I do not like.

My love,
understand me,
I want you all,
from your eyes to your feet, your toenails,
the inside of you,
all the clarity which you preserved.

It is I, my love,
knocking at your door.
It is not the ghost, it is not
the one who used to stand
at your window.
I beat the door down;
I come into all your life;
I am coming to live in your soul;
you can do nothing against me.

Tienes que abrir puerta a puerta,
tienes que obedecerme,
tienes que abrir los ojos
para que busque en ellos,
tienes que ver cómo ando
con pasos pesados
por todos los caminos
que, ciegos, me esperaban.

No me temas,
soy tuyo,
pero
no soy el pasajero ni el mendigo,
soy tu dueño,
el que tú esperabas,
y ahora entro
en tu vida,
para no salir más,
amor, amor, amor,
para quedarme.

You have to open door after door,
you have to obey me,
you have to open your eyes
so that I can search them,
you have to see how I walk
with heavy steps
along all the paths
which blindly awaited me.

Do not be afraid of me,
I am yours,
but
I am not a passer-by nor a beggar,
I am your master,
the one you were waiting for,
and now I am coming
into your life,
never to leave it again,
my love, my love, my love,
to stay for ever.

La pródiga

Yo te escogí entre todas las mujeres
para que repitieras
sobre la tierra
mi corazón que baila con espigas
o lucha sin cuartel cuando hace falta.

Yo te pregunto, dónde está mi hijo?

No me esperaba en ti, reconociéndome,
y diciéndome: 'Llámame para salir sobre la tierra
a continuar tus luchas y tus cantos'?

Devuélveme a mi hijo!

Lo has olvidado en las puertas
del placer, oh pródiga
enemiga,
has olvidado que viniste a esta cita,
la más profunda, aquella
en que los dos, unidos, seguiremos hablando
por su boca, amor mío,
ay todo aquello
que no alcanzamos a decirnos?

Cuando yo te levanto en una ola
de fuego y sangre, y se duplica
la vida entre nosotros,
acuérdate
que alguien nos llama

The Prodigal

I picked you out among all women
so that you would echo
on earth
my heart which dances with the corn
or fights without mercy when there is need.

I ask you, where is my son?

Was he not waiting for me in you, knowing me
and saying to me: 'Call me out onto the earth
to carry on your struggles and your songs'?

Give me back my son!

Have you left him at the doors
of pleasure, you prodigal
enemy,
have you forgotten that you came to this meeting,
the most important one, the one
in which we two, united, will speak on
through his mouth, my love,
ah, everything
that we could find no way to tell each other?

When I lift you on a wave
of fire and blood, and life
is doubled between us,
remember
that someone is calling us

como nadie jamás nos ha llamado,
y que no respondemos
y nos quedamos solos y cobardes
ante la vida que negamos.

Pródiga,
abre las puertas,
y que en tu corazón
el nudo ciego
se desenlace y vuele
con tu sangre y la mía
por el mundo!

as no one ever called us before,
and that we are not answering
and that we stand as lonely cowards
before the life that we deny.

Prodigal,
open the doors,
and in your heart
let the knot of blindness
be untied, let it fly
with your blood and mine
throughout the world!

El daño

Te he hecho daño, alma mía,
he desgarrado tu alma.

Entiéndeme.
Todos saben quién soy,
pero ese Soy
es además un hombre
para ti.

En ti vacilo, caigo
y me levanto ardiendo.
Tú entre todos los seres
tienes derecho
a verme débil.
Y tu pequeña mano
de pan y de guitarra
debe tocar mi pecho
cuando sale al combate.

Por eso busco en ti la firme piedra.
Asperas manos en tu sangre clavo
buscando tu firmeza
y la profundidad que necesito,
y si no encuentro
sino tu risa de metal, si no hallo
nada en qué sostener mis duros pasos,
adorada, recibe
mi tristeza y mi cólera,
mis manos enemigas

The Hurt

I have hurt you, sweetheart,
I have broken your heart.

Understand me.
Everyone knows who I am,
but this I-am
is also a man
for you.

In you I hesitate, I fall
and rise up burning.
You among all beings
have the right
to see me weak.
And your little hand
made for bread and the guitar
must touch my breast
when it goes out to fight.

For this I seek in you solid rock.
I thrust my rough hands into your blood
seeking your firmness
and the depth that I need,
and if I find only
your metallic laugh, if I trace nothing
on which my hard feet can stand firm,
beloved, then take
my sadness and my anger,
my hostile hands

destruyéndote un poco
para que te levantes de la arcilla,
hecha de nuevo para mis combates.

which will destroy you a little
so that you rise up out of the clay,
made anew for my battles.

El pozo

A veces te hundes, caes
en tu agujero de silencio,
en tu abismo de cólera orgullosa,
y apenas puedes
volver, aún con jirones
de lo que hallaste
en la profundidad de tu existencia.

Amor mío, qué encuentras
en tu pozo cerrado?
Algas, ciénagas, rocas?
Qué ves con ojos ciegos,
rencorosa y herida?

Mi vida, no hallarás
en el pozo en que caes
lo que yo guardo para ti en la altura:
un ramo de jazmines con rocío,
un beso más profundo que tu abismo.

No me temas, no caigas
en tu rencor de nuevo.
Sacude la palabra mía que vino a herirte
y déjala que vuele por la ventana abierta.
Ella volverá a herirme
sin que tú la dirijas
puesto que fue cargada con un instante duro
y ese instante será desarmado en mi pecho.

The Well

Sometimes you plunge, you fall
into your hole of silence,
into your abyss of proud anger,
and you are scarcely able
to return, still hampered by
the scraps of what you find
in the depths of your existence.

O my love, what do you find
at the bottom of your secret well?
Seaweed, boggy marsh, or rocks?
What do you see with your blind eyes
when full of wounded rancour?

O my life, you will not find,
when you fall into your well,
what I keep for you on the surface:
a branch of jasmine flowers with dew,
a kiss yet deeper than your abyss.

Do not fear me, do not fall
back again into your rancour.
Shake off my words that came to hurt you
and let them fly off through the open window.
They will return to hurt me then
without your having to direct them
for they were loaded with a moment's harshness
and that moment will be softened in my breast.

Sonríeme radiosa
si mi boca te hiere.
No soy un pastor dulce
como en los cuentos de hadas,
sino un buen leñador que comparte contigo
tierra, viento y espinas de los montes.

Amame, tú, sonríeme,
ayúdame a ser bueno.
No te hieras en mí, que será inútil,
no me hieras a mí porque te hieres.

Give me a radiant smile
if my mouth hurts you.
I am not a gentle shepherd
like you find in fairy tales,
but rather a good lumberjack who shares with you
the earth, the wind and thorns on the mountains.

Love me, you must, smile at me,
help me to be good.
Do not hurt yourself in me, that would be pointless,
do not hurt me because you hurt yourself.

El sueño

Andando en las arenas
yo decidí dejarte.

Pisaba un barro oscuro
que temblaba,
y hundiéndome y saliendo
decidí que salieras
de mí, que me pesabas
como piedra cortante,
y elaboré tu pérdida
paso a paso:
cortarte las raíces,
soltarte sola al viento.

Ay en ese minuto,
corazón mío, un sueño
con sus alas terribles
te cubría.

Te sentías tragada por el barro,
y me llamabas y yo no acudía,

te ibas, inmóvil,
sin defenderte
hasta ahogarte en la boca de arena.

Después
mi decisión se encontró con tu sueño,
y desde la ruptura

The Dream

Walking over the sands
I decided to leave you.

I stepped on a dark quicksand
that quivered,
and sinking in and climbing out
I decided that you should climb out
of me, that you were weighing me down
like a jagged stone,
and I planned how to lose you,
step by step:
to cut off your roots,
cast you out to the wind.

Ah, in that minute,
my heart, a dream
covered you in
with its terrible wings.

You felt yourself swallowed up by the quicksand,
and you called me and I did not come to help,

you sank, unmoving,
without a struggle,
until you were smothered in the sandy mouth.

Later
my decision came together with your dream,
and out of the break

que nos quebraba el alma,
surgimos limpios otra vez, desnudos,
amándonos
sin sueño, sin arena,
completos y radiantes,
sellados por el fuego.

which shattered our souls
we rose up again, cleansed and naked,
loving again
without dreams, without sands,
complete and radiant,
sealed by fire.

Si tú me olvidas

Quiero que sepas
una cosa.

Tú sabes cómo es esto:
si miro
la luna de cristal, la rama roja
del lento otoño en mi ventana,
si toco
junto al fuego
la impalpable ceniza
o el arrugado cuerpo de la leña,
todo me lleva a ti,
como si todo lo que existe,
aromas, luz, metales,
fueran pequeños barcos que navegan
hacia las islas tuyas que me aguardan.

Ahora bien,
si poco a poco dejas de quererme
dejaré de quererte poco a poco.

Si de pronto
me olvidas
no me busques,
que ya te habré olvidado.

Si consideras largo y loco
el viento de banderas
que pasa por mi vida

If You Forget Me

I want you to know
one thing.

You know how it is:
if I look at
the crystal moon, the red branch
of slow autumn in my window,
if I touch
next to the fire
the insubstantial ashes
or the wrinkled body of a piece of wood,
everything brings me back to you,
as if everything that existed,
perfumes, light, metals,
were little boats steering their way
towards your islands which await me.

But nonetheless,
if little by little you stop loving me
I shall stop loving you, little by little.

If suddenly
you forget me
do not look for me,
for I shall already have forgotten you.

If you consider the wind of banners
that waves through my life
to be loose and crazy

y te decides
a dejarme a la orilla
del corazón en que tengo raíces,
piensa
que en ese día,
a esa hora
levantaré los brazos
y saldrán mis raíces
a buscar otra tierra.

Pero
si cada día,
cada hora
sientes que a mí estás destinada
con dulzura implacable.
Si cada día sube
una flor a tus labios a buscarme,
ay amor mío, ay mía,
en mí todo ese fuego se repite,
en mí nada se apaga ni se olvida,
mi amor se nutre de tu amor, amada,
y mientras vivas estará en tus brazos
sin salir de los míos.

and you decide
to leave me on the edge
of the heart in which I have my roots,
then think
that on that very day,
at that very minute,
I shall lift up my arms
and take up my roots
to look for new ground.

But
if every day,
every minute,
you feel that you are destined for me
with relentless sweetness,
if every day a flower
rises to your lips in search of me,
ah, my love, ah, my own,
in me all this fire is repeated,
in me nothing is extinguished or forgotten,
my love feeds on your love, beloved,
and while you live it will be in your arms
without leaving mine.

El olvido

Todo el amor en una copa
ancha como la tierra, todo
el amor con estrellas y espinas
te di, pero anduviste
con pies pequeños, con tacones sucios
sobre el fuego, apagándolo.

Ay gran amor, pequeña amada!

No me detuve en la lucha.
No dejé de marchar hacia la vida,
hacia la paz, hacia el pan para todos,
pero te alcé en mis brazos
y te clavé a mis besos
y te miré como jamás
volverán a mirarte ojos humanos.

Ay gran amor, pequeña amada!

Entonces no mediste mi estatura,
y al hombre que para ti apartó
la sangre, el trigo, el agua
confundiste
con el pequeño insecto que te cayó en la falda.

Ay gran amor, pequeña amada!

No esperes que te mire en la distancia
hacia atrás, permanece

Forgetting

The whole of love in one glass
wide as the world, the whole
of love with stars and thorns
I gave you, but you walked
on my fire with little feet,
with dirty heels, stamping it out.

What a great love, what a small beloved!

I did not pause in the struggle.
I did not cease to march towards life,
towards peace, towards bread for all,
but I lifted you up in my arms
and I nailed you to my kisses
and I gazed on you as never
human eyes will gaze on you again.

What a great love, what a small beloved!

Then you did not know the measure of my stature,
and the man who for you procured
blood, wheat, water
you confused
with the little insect that fell into your lap.

What a great love, what a small beloved!

Do not expect me to look back at you
from afar, stay

con lo que te dejé, pasea
con mi fotografía traicionada,
yo seguiré marchando,
abriendo anchos caminos contra la sombra, haciendo
suave la tierra, repartiendo
la estrella para los que vienen.

Quédate en el camino.
Ha llegado la noche para ti.
Tal vez de madrugada
nos veremos de nuevo.

Ay gran amor, pequeña amada!

with what I left you, walk
with my betrayed photograph,
I shall still march on,
opening up wide roads against the darkness,
making the earth sweet, sharing out
the star for those still to come.

Stay behind on the road.
Night has arrived for you.
Perhaps in the morning light
we shall meet again.

What a great love, what a small beloved!

Las muchachas

Muchachas que buscabais
el gran amor, el gran amor terrible,
qué ha pasado, muchachas?

Tal vez
el tiempo, el tiempo!

Porque ahora,
aquí está, ved cómo pasa
arrastrando las piedras celestes,
destrozando las flores y las hojas,
con un ruido de espumas azotadas
contra todas las piedras de tu mundo,
con un olor de esperma y de jazmines,
junto a la luna sangrienta!

Y ahora
tocas el agua con tus pies pequeños,
con tu pequeño corazón
y no sabes qué hacer!

Son mejores
ciertos viajes nocturnos,
ciertos departamentos,
ciertos divertidísimos paseos,
ciertos bailes sin mayor consecuencia
que continuar el viaje!

Muérete de miedo o de frío,
o de duda,

Girls

Girls, you who were looking for
the great love, the great and terrible love,
what happened, girls?

Perhaps
time, just time!

For now,
here it is, see how it passes by,
hauling away the stones of heaven,
mangling the flowers and leaves,
with the noise of foam lashing
against all the stones of your world,
with a smell of sperm and jasmine,
close by the bleeding moon!

And now
you touch the water with your little feet
with your little heart,
and you do not know what to do!

It is better to enjoy
certain voyages by night,
certain compartments,
certain entertaining walks,
certain dances of no great consequence,
better than to continue the journey!

Die of fear or of cold,
or of doubt,

que yo con mis grandes pasos
la encontraré,
dentro de ti
o lejos de ti,
y ella me encontrará,
la que no temblará frente al amor,
la que estará fundida
conmigo
en la vida o la muerte!

but I with my long strides
shall find her,
inside of you
or far from you,
and she will find me,
she who will not tremble in the face of love,
she who will be fused
with me
in life or in death!

Tú venías

No me has hecho sufrir
sino esperar.

Aquellas horas
enmarañadas, llenas
de serpientes,
cuando
se me caía el alma y me ahogaba,
tú venías andando,
tú venías desnuda y arañada,
tú llegabas sangrienta hasta mi lecho,
novia mía,
y entonces
toda la noche caminamos
durmiendo
y cuando despertamos
eras intacta y nueva,
como si el grave viento de los sueños
de nuevo hubiera dado
fuego a tu cabellera
y en trigo y plata hubiera sumergido
tu cuerpo hasta dejarlo deslumbrante.

Yo no sufrí, amor mío,
yo sólo te esperaba.
Tenías que cambiar de corazón
y de mirada
después de haber tocado la profunda
zona de mar que te entregó mi pecho.

You Came

You did not make me suffer,
you made me hope.

In those hours
of confusion, full
of serpents,
when
my courage failed me and I drowned,
you came along,
you came naked and covered in scratches,
you arrived bleeding at my bed,
my bride,
and then
we walked all night
in our sleep
and when we awoke
you were whole again and new,
as if the blustery wind of dreams
had given fresh
fire to your hair
and had dipped your body in wheat
and silver to leave it dazzling bright.

I did not suffer, my love,
I waited only for you.
You had to change your heart
and your way of looking
once you had touched the deep zone
of the sea which my breast gave you.

Tenías que salir del agua
pura como una gota levantada
por una ola nocturna.

Novia mía, tuviste
que morir y nacer, yo te esperaba.
Yo no sufrí buscándote,
sabía que vendrías,
una nueva mujer con lo que adoro
de la que no adoraba,
con tus ojos, tus manos y tu boca
pero con otro corazón
que amaneció a mi lado
como si siempre hubiera estado allí
para seguir conmigo para siempre.

You had to come out of the water
as pure as a drop lifted up
by a wave at night.

My bride, you had to die
and be reborn, I waited for you.
I did not suffer while I sought you,
I knew that you would come,
a new woman, with what I adored
of the one I did not adore,
with your eyes, your hands and your mouth
but with a different heart
which awoke at my side
as if it had always been there
to be my companion for ever.

Human Lives

Las vidas

El monte y el río

En mi patria hay un monte.
En mi patria hay un río.

Ven conmigo.

La noche al monte sube.
El hambre baja al río.

Ven conmigo.

Quiénes son los que sufren?
No sé, pero son míos.

Ven conmigo.

No sé, pero me llaman
y me dicen 'Sufrimos'.

Ven conmigo.

Y me dicen: 'Tu pueblo,
tu pueblo desdichado,
entre el monte y el río,

con hambre y con dolores,
no quiere luchar solo,
te está esperando, amigo'.

The Mountain and the River

In my country there is a mountain.
In my country there is a river.

Come with me.

Night is climbing up the mountain.
Hunger is going down to the river.

Come with me.

Who are those that suffer?
I do not know, but they are mine.

Come with me.

I do not know, but they call me
and say to me 'We are suffering'.

Come with me.

And they say to me: 'Your people,
your unhappy people,
between the mountain and the river,

suffering hunger and pain,
do not want to struggle alone,
we are waiting for you, friend'.

Oh tú, la que yo amo,
pequeña, grano rojo
de trigo,

será dura la lucha,
la vida será dura,
pero vendrás conmigo.

Oh, you that I love,
my little one, my red
grain of wheat,

the struggle will be hard,
our life will be hard,
but you will come with me.

La pobreza

Ay no quieres,
te asusta
la pobreza,

no quieres
ir con zapatos rotos al mercado
y volver con el viejo vestido.

Amor, no amamos,
como quieren los ricos,
la miseria. Nosotros
la extirparemos como diente maligno
que hasta ahora ha mordido el corazón del hombre.

Pero no quiero
que la temas.
Si llega por mi culpa a tu morada,
si la pobreza expulsa
tus zapatos dorados,
que no expulse tu risa que es el pan de mi vida.
Si no puedes pagar el alquiler
sal al trabajo con paso orgulloso,
y piensa, amor, que yo te estoy mirando
y somos juntos la mayor riqueza
que jamás se reunió sobre la tierra.

Poverty

Ah, you do not like it,
you are frightened
by poverty,

you do not like
going to market with torn shoes
and coming back with your old dress.

My love, we do not love
misery, as the rich
would like us to. We shall
root it out like a rotten tooth
which until now has been eating away the heart of man.

But I do not want
you to fear it.
If by my fault it should enter your household,
if poverty should throw out
your golden shoes,
let it not throw out your laugh, the bread of my life.
If you cannot pay the rent
go out to work with pride in your step,
and think, my love, that I can see you
and we are together the greatest wealth
that was ever amassed on this earth.

Las vidas

Ay qué incómoda a veces
te siento
conmigo, vencedor entre los hombres!

Porque no sabes
que conmigo vencieron
miles de rostros que no puedes ver,
miles de pies y pechos que marcharon conmigo,
que no soy,
que no existo,
que sólo soy la frente de los que van conmigo,
que soy más fuerte
porque llevo en mí
no mi pequeña vida
sino todas las vidas,
y ando seguro hacia adelante
porque tengo mil ojos,
golpeo con peso de piedra
porque tengo mil manos
y mi voz se oye en las orillas
de todas las tierras
porque es la voz de todos
los que no hablaron,
de los que no cantaron
y cantan hoy con esta boca
que a ti te besa.

Human Lives

Ah how uncomfortable I feel you are
sometimes
with me, a conqueror among men!

Because you do not know
that with me were victorious
thousands of faces that you cannot see,
thousands of feet and breasts that marched with me,
that I am not,
that I do not exist,
that I am only the head of those that go with me,
that I am stronger
because I bear within me
not my tiny life
but all human lives,
and I stride forward in safety
because I have a thousand eyes,
I strike with the weight of rock
because I have a thousand hands
and my voice is heard on the shores
of all the lands on earth
because it is the voice of all
those that did not speak,
of those that did not sing
and who sing today with this mouth
which kisses you.

La bandera

Levántate conmigo.

Nadie quisiera
como yo quedarse
sobre la almohada en que tus párpados
quieren cerrar el mundo para mí.
Allí también quisiera
dejar dormir mi sangre
rodeando tu dulzura.

Pero levántate,
tú, levántate,
pero conmigo levántate
y salgamos reunidos
a luchar cuerpo a cuerpo
contra las telarañas del malvado,
contra el sistema que reparte el hambre,
contra la organización de la miseria.

Vamos,
y tú, mi estrella, junto a mí,
recién nacida de mi propia arcilla,
ya habrás hallado el manantial que ocultas
y en medio del fuego estarás
junto a mí,
con tus ojos bravíos,
alzando mi bandera.

The Banner

Rise up with me.

Nobody would like
more than I to stay here
on the pillow where your eyelids
seek to close in the world for me.
There I too should like
to let my blood sleep
encircling your sweetness.

But rise up,
you must, rise up,
rise up now with me
and let us go out together
to fight hand to hand
against the cobwebs of the wicked,
against the system that doles out hunger,
against the organisation of misery.

Let us go,
and you, my star, together with me,
newly born from my own clay,
you will already have found the spring that you hide
and in the middle of the fire you will be
together with me,
with your fierce eyes,
raising up my banner.

El amor del soldado

En plena guerra te llevó la vida
a ser el amor del soldado.

Con tu pobre vestido de seda,
tus uñas de piedra falsa
te tocó caminar por el fuego.

Ven acá, vagabunda,
ven a beber sobre mi pecho
rojo rocío.

No querías saber dónde andabas,
eras la compañera de baile,
no tenías partido ni patria.

Y ahora a mi lado caminando
ves que conmigo va la vida
y que detrás está la muerte.

Ya no puedes volver a bailar
con tu traje de seda en la sala.

Te vas a romper los zapatos,
pero vas a crecer en la marcha.

Tienes que andar sobre las espinas
dejando gotitas de sangre.

Bésame de nuevo, querida.

Limpia ese fusil, camarada.

A Soldier's Love

In the middle of war life led you
to be a soldier's love.

With your poor silk dress,
your nails of imitation stones
it was your lot to go through gunfire.

Come here, vagabond,
come and drink at my breast
red dew.

You did not want to know where you were going,
you were the dancing partner,
you had no party and no motherland.

And now that you are walking by my side
you see that life goes with me
and that behind me is death.

Now you cannot go back to the dance
in the hall, with your silk ballgown.

You will ruin your shoes,
but you will grow on the march.

You have to walk on thorns
leaving drops of your blood.

Kiss me again, beloved.

Clean that rifle, comrade.

No sólo el fuego

Ay sí, recuerdo,
ay tus ojos cerrados
como llenos por dentro de luz negra,
todo tu cuerpo como una mano abierta,
como un racimo blanco de la luna,
y el éxtasis,
cuando nos mata un rayo,
cuando un puñal nos hiere en las raíces
y nos rompe una luz la cabellera,
y cuando
vamos de nuevo
volviendo a la vida,
como si del océano saliéramos,
como si del naufragio
volviéramos heridos
entre las piedras y las algas rojas.

Pero
hay otros recuerdos,
no sólo flores del incendio,
sino pequeños brotes
que aparecen de pronto
cuando voy en los trenes
o en las calles.

Te veo
lavando mis pañuelos,
colgando en la ventana
mis calcetines rotos,

Not Only Fire

Ah yes, I remember,
ah, your eyes closed
as if filled inside with black light,
your whole body like an open hand,
like a white shape from the moon,
and the ecstasy,
when a lightning flash strikes us dead,
when a dagger wounds us in our roots
and a light breaks through our hair,
and when
we return
to life again,
as if we were emerging from the ocean,
as if from a shipwreck
we were returning injured
among the rocks and red seaweed.

But
there are other memories,
not only flowers of fire,
but little buds
which suddenly appear
when I go on trains
or through the streets.

I see you
washing my handkerchieves,
hanging in the window
my worn-out socks,

tu figura en que todo,
todo el placer como una llamarada
cayó sin destruirte,
de nuevo,
mujercita
de cada día,
de nuevo ser humano,
humildemente humano,
soberbiamente pobre,
como tienes que ser para que seas
no la rápida rosa
que la ceniza del amor deshace,
sino toda la vida,
toda la vida con jabón y agujas,
con el aroma que amo
de la cocina que tal vez no tendremos
y en que tu mano entre las papas fritas
y tu boca cantando en invierno
mientras llega el asado
serían para mí la permanencia
de la felicidad sobre la tierra.

Ay vida mía,
no sólo el fuego entre nosotros arde,
sino toda la vida,
la simple historia,
el simple amor
de una mujer y un hombre
parecidos a todos.

your figure into which
all pleasure like a sudden flare
fell without destroying you,
again,
my ordinary
little woman,
once again a human being,
meekly human,
magnificently poor,
as you have to be so that you are not
the fleeting rose
destroyed by the ashes of love,
but rather the whole of life,
the whole of life with soap and needles,
with the smell that I love
of the kitchen that perhaps we shall not have
and in which your hand among the fried potatoes
and your mouth singing in winter
while the roast is cooking
would be for me everlasting
happiness on this earth.

Ah, love of my life,
not only fire burns between us,
but the whole of life,
the simple story,
the simple love
of a woman and a man
the same as all the others.

La muerta

Si de pronto no existes,
si de pronto no vives,
yo seguiré viviendo.

No me atrevo,
no me atrevo a escribirlo,
si te mueres.

Yo seguiré viviendo.

Porque donde no tiene voz un hombre
allí, mi voz.

Donde los negros sean apaleados,
yo no puedo estar muerto.
Cuando entren en la cárcel mis hermanos
entraré yo con ellos.

Cuando la victoria,
no mi victoria,
sino la gran victoria
llegue,
aunque esté mudo debo hablar:
yo la veré llegar aunque esté ciego.

No, perdóname.
Si tú no vives,
si tú, querida, amor mío,
si tú

Dead Woman

If suddenly you do not exist,
if suddenly you no longer live,
I shall live on.

I do not dare,
I do not dare to write it,
if you die.

I shall live on.

For where a man has no voice,
there shall be my voice.

Where blacks are flogged and beaten,
I cannot be dead.
When my brothers go to prison
I shall go with them.

When victory,
not my victory,
but the great victory
comes,
even if I am dumb I must speak;
I shall see it coming even if I am blind.

No, forgive me.
If you no longer live,
if you, beloved, my love,
if you

te has muerto,
todas las hojas caerán en mi pecho,
lloverá sobre mi alma noche y día,
la nieve quemará mi corazón,
andaré con frío y fuego y muerte y nieve,
mis pies querrán marchar hacia donde tú duermes,
pero
seguiré vivo,
porque tú me quisiste sobre todas las cosas
indomable,
y, amor, porque tú sabes que soy no sólo un hombre
sino todos los hombres.

have died,
all the leaves will fall on my breast,
it will rain on my soul night and day,
the snow will burn my heart,
I shall walk with frost and fire and death and snow,
my feet will want to walk to where you are sleeping,
but
I shall stay alive,
because above all things you wanted me
indomitable,
and, my love, because you know that I am not only a man
but all mankind.

Pequeña América

Cuando miro la forma
de América en el mapa,
amor, a ti te veo:
las alturas del cobre en tu cabeza,
tus pechos, trigo y nieve,
tu cintura delgada,
veloces ríos que palpitan, dulces
colinas y praderas
y en el frío del sur tus pies terminan
su geografía de oro duplicado.

Amor, cuando te toco
no sólo han recorrido
mis manos tu delicia,
sino ramas y tierra, frutas y agua,
la primavera que amo,
la luna del desierto, el pecho
de la paloma salvaje,
la suavidad de las piedras gastadas
por las aguas del mar o de los ríos
y la espesura roja
del matorral en donde
la sed y el hambre acechan.
Y así mi patria extensa me recibe,
pequeña América, en tu cuerpo.

Aún más, cuando te veo recostada
veo en tu piel, en tu color de avena,
la nacionalidad de mi cariño.

Little America

When I look at the shape
of America on the map,
my love, it is you that I see;
the mountains of copper in your hair,
your breasts, wheat and snow,
your delicate waist,
rushing rivers that throb, sweet
hills and meadows
and your feet in the cold of the south complete
its geography of duplicated gold.

My love, when I touch you
my hands not only travel
across the delights of your body,
but over branches and earth, fruits and water,
through the spring that I love,
the moon in the desert, the breast
of the wild dove,
the softness of stones worn away
by the waters of the sea or of rivers
and over the red thicket
of the brushwood where
thirst and hunger lie in wait.
And so my vast motherland welcomes me,
my little America, in your body.

Even more, when I see you lying down
I see in your skin, in your colour of oats,
the nationality of my love.

Porque desde tus hombros
el cortador de caña
de Cuba abrasadora
me mira, lleno de sudor oscuro,
y desde tu garganta
pescadores que tiemblan
en las húmedas casas de la orilla
me cantan su secreto.
Y así a lo largo de tu cuerpo,
pequeña América adorada,
las tierras y los pueblos
interrumpen mis besos
y tu belleza entonces
no sólo enciende el fuego
que arde sin consumirse entre nosotros,
sino que con tu amor me está llamando
y a través de tu vida
me está dando la vida que me falta
y al sabor de tu amor se agrega el barro,
el beso de la tierra que me aguarda.

Because from your shoulders
the sugar-cane cutter
from scorching Cuba
looks out at me, covered with dark sweat,
and from your throat
fishermen shivering
in damp houses by the seashore
sing me their secret.
And so along the length of your body,
my adorable little America,
the lands and the peoples
interrupt my kisses
and then your beauty
not only lights the fire
that burns between us, never dying,
but also calls to me with your love
and through your life
gives me the life that I was lacking,
and to the taste of your love is joined the clay,
the kiss of the earth which awaits me.

Ode and Germinating Seeds

Oda y germinaciones

I

El sabor de tu boca y el color de tu piel,
piel, boca, fruta mía de estos días veloces,
dímelo, fueron sin cesar a tu lado
por años y por viajes y por lunas y soles
y tierra y llanto y lluvia y alegría
o sólo ahora, sólo
salen de tus raíces
como a la tierra seca el agua trae
germinaciones que no conocía
o a los labios del cántaro olvidado
sube en el agua el gusto de la tierra?

No sé, no me lo digas, no lo sabes.
Nadie sabe estas cosas.
Pero acercando todos mis sentidos
a la luz de tu piel, desapareces,
te fundes como el ácido
aroma de una fruta
y el calor de un camino,
el olor del maíz que se desgrana,
la madreselva de la tarde pura,
los nombres de la tierra polvorienta,
el perfume infinito de la patria:
magnolia y matorral, sangre y harina,
galope de caballos,
la luna polvorienta de la aldea,
el pan recién nacido:
ay todo de tu piel vuelve a mi boca,
vuelve a mi corazón, vuelve a mi cuerpo,

I

The taste of your mouth and the colour of your skin,
skin, mouth, my fruit of these fleeting days,
tell me, were they always with you
through the years and journeys, moons and suns,
and earth and weeping and rain and joy,
or do they only now
sprout forth from your roots
as from dry earth water draws out
germinating seeds the earth did not know
or in water from a forgotten pitcher
the taste of the earth rises to the lips?

I do not know, do not tell me, you do not know.
No one knows these things.
But drawing all my senses
to the light of your skin, you disappear,
you melt like the acid
perfume of a fruit
or the heat of the road,
the smell of maize as it drops its seeds,
honeysuckle on a clear evening,
the names of earth as it turns to dust,
the infinite perfume of the motherland:
magnolia and brushwood, blood and flour,
the galloping of horses,
the dusty moon over the village,
newborn bread;
ah, everything about your skin comes back to my mouth,
comes back to my heart, comes back to my body,

y vuelvo a ser contigo
la tierra que tú eres:
eres en mí profunda primavera:
vuelvo a saber en ti cómo germino.

and with you I am again
the earth that you are.
You are in me the essence of spring;
in you I learn again how I germinate.

II

Años tuyos que yo debí sentir
crecer cerca de mí como racimos
hasta que hubieras visto cómo el sol y la tierra
a mis manos de piedra te hubieran destinado,
hasta que uva con uva hubieras hecho
cantar en mis venas el vino.
El viento o el caballo
desviándose pudieron
hacer que yo pasara por tu infancia,
el mismo cielo has visto cada día,
el mismo barro del invierno oscuro,
la enramada sin fin de los ciruelos
y su dulzura de color morado.
Sólo algunos kilómetros de noche,
las distancias mojadas
de la aurora campestre,
un puñado de tierra nos separó, los muros
transparentes
que no cruzamos, para que la vida,
después, pusiera todos
los mares y la tierra
entre nosotros, y nos acercáramos
a pesar del espacio,
paso a paso buscándonos,
de un océano a otro,
hasta que vi que el cielo se incendiaba
y volaba en la luz tu cabellera
y llegaste a mis besos con el fuego
de un desencadenado meteoro

I I

Your years which I should have felt
growing next to me like bunches of grapes
until you had seen how the sun and the earth
had intended you for my hands of stone,
until from grape to grape you had made
the wine sing in my veins.
The wind or a horse
losing its way
could have sent me riding through your childhood,
you saw the same sky each day,
the same mud in the darkness of winter,
the endless foliage of the plum trees
and their purple-coloured sweetness.
Only a few kilometres of night,
the moist distances
of dawn in the countryside,
a handful of earth separated us,
transparent walls
we did not cross, so that life
later put between us
the seas and the earth,
and we came to each other
in spite of space,
seeking each other step by step,
from one ocean to another,
until I saw the heavens catching fire
and in the light saw your hair soaring
and you came to my kisses with the fire
of an unchained meteor

y al fundirte en mi sangre, la dulzura
del ciruelo salvaje
de nuestra infancia recibí en mi boca,
y te apreté a mi pecho como
si la tierra y la vida recobrara.

and as you melted into my blood, the sweetness
of the wild plum tree
of our childhood came into my mouth,
and I hugged you to my breast as if
restored to earth and life.

III

Mi muchacha salvaje, hemos tenido
que recobrar el tiempo
y marchar hacia atrás, en la distancia
de nuestras vidas, beso a beso,
recogiendo de un sitio lo que dimos
sin alegría, descubriendo en otro
el camino secreto
que iba acercando tus pies a los míos,
y así bajo mi boca
vuelves a ver la planta insatisfecha
de tu vida alargando sus raíces
hacia mi corazón que te esperaba.
Y una a una las noches
entre nuestras ciudades separadas
se agregan a la noche que nos une.
La luz de cada día
su llama o su reposo
nos entregan, sacándolos del tiempo,
y así se desentierra
en la sombra o la luz nuestro tesoro,
y así besan la vida nuestros besos:
todo el amor en nuestro amor se encierra:
toda la sed termina en nuestro abrazo.
Aquí estamos al fin frente a frente,
nos hemos encontrado,
no hemos perdido nada.
Nos hemos recorrido labio a labio,
hemos cambiado mil veces
entre nosotros la muerte y la vida,

III

My wild maiden, we have had to
make up for lost time
and walk back into the distance
of our lives, kiss by kiss,
collecting from some place all the things we gave
without joy, discovering in another
the secret path
which gradually led your feet to mine,
and so under my mouth
you come to see again the unsatisfied plant
of your life spreading out its roots
towards my heart, which has been waiting for you.
And one by one the nights
between our separated cities
join with the night which makes us one.
The light of each day
gives us its fire or its peace,
stealing them from Time,
and so our treasure
is dug up in darkness or in light,
and so life is kissed by our kisses;
all love is enclosed in our love;
all thirst is slaked in our embrace.
Here we are at last, face to face,
we have found each other,
we have lost nothing.
We have travelled through each other lip by lip,
we have exchanged a thousand times
death and life with one another,

todo lo que traíamos
como muertas medallas
lo echamos al fondo del mar,
todo lo que aprendimos
no nos sirvió de nada:
comenzamos de nuevo,
terminamos de nuevo
muerte y vida.
Y aquí sobrevivimos,
puros, con la pureza que nosotros creamos,
más anchos que la tierra que no pudo extraviarnos,
eternos como el fuego que arderá
cuanto dure la vida.

everything we brought with us
like lifeless medals
we cast into the depths of the sea,
everything we had learned
was no use to us at all;
we are making a new start,
we are making a new end
to death and life.
And here we survive,
pure, with the purity that we create,
wider than the earth which could not lead us astray
eternal as the fire which will burn
as long as life shall last.

IV

Cuando he llegado aquí se detiene mi mano.
Alguien pregunta: – Díme por qué, como las olas
en una misma costa, tus palabras
sin cesar van y vuelven a su cuerpo?
Ella es sólo la forma que tú amas?
Y respondo: mis manos no se sacian
en ella, mis besos no descansan,
por qué retiraría las palabras
que repiten la huella de su contacto amado,
que se cierran guardando
inútilmente como en la red el agua,
la superficie y la temperatura
de la ola más pura de la vida?
Y, amor, tu cuerpo no sólo es la rosa
que en la sombra o la luna se levanta,
o sorprendo o persigo.
No sólo es movimiento o quemadura,
acto de sangre o pétalo del fuego,
sino que para mí tú me has traído
mi territorio, el barro de mi infancia,
las olas de la avena,
la piel redonda de la fruta oscura
que arranqué de la selva,
aroma de maderas y manzanas,
color de agua escondida donde caen
frutos secretos y profundas hojas.
Oh amor, tu cuerpo sube
como una línea pura de vasija
desde la tierra que me reconoce

I V

Having arrived at this point, my hand stops.
Someone asks: 'Tell me why your words,
like waves keeping to the same coast,
ceaselessly ebb and flow back to her body?
Is she the only physical form that you love?'
And I answer: 'My hands never have enough
of her, my kisses never tire,
why should I take back the words
which recall the trace of her beloved touch,
which close in a guardian circle
as uselessly as a net to catch water,
to preserve the surface and the temperature
of the purest of all the waves of life?'
And, love, your body is not only the rose
growing in the darkness or the moonlight,
which I chance upon or seek.
It is not only movement or burning,
a bloody deed or a petal of fire,
but also it was you who brought to me
my homeland, the clay soil of my childhood,
the waves across the oatfields,
the round skin of the dark fruit
that I tore from the jungle,
the smell of wood and of apples,
the colour of hidden waters where secret fruits
and deep leaves fall.
Oh love, your body rises
like the clean lines of a pot
from the land which knows me well,

y cuando te encontraron mis sentidos
tú palpitaste como si cayeran
dentro de ti la lluvia y las semillas!
Ay que me digan cómo
pudiera yo abolirte
y dejar que mis manos sin tu forma
arrancaran el fuego a mis palabras!
Suave mía, reposa
tu cuerpo en estas líneas que te deben
más de lo que me das en tu contacto,
vive en estas palabras y repite
en ellas la dulzura y el incendio,
estremécete en medio de sus sílabas,
duerme en mi nombre como te has dormido
sobre mi corazón, y así mañana
el hueco de tu forma
guardarán mis palabras
y el que las oiga un día recibirá una ráfaga
de trigo y amapolas:
estará todavía respirando
el cuerpo del amor sobre la tierra!

and while my senses were discovering you
you quivered as if inside you
rain and seeds were falling down!
Ah, let them tell me how
I could get rid of you
and stop my hands without your body
from drawing fire from my words!
My sweet love, lay your body
down on these lines which owe you
more than what you give me by your touch,
live in these words and recreate
in them the sweetness and the fire,
shiver in the midst of their syllables,
sleep in my name as you slept
next to my heart, and so tomorrow
my words will preserve
the impression of your form
and the man who one day hears them will feel a gust
of wheat and poppies;
and still the body will be breathing,
the body of love on this earth!

V

Hilo de trigo y agua,
de cristal o de fuego,
la palabra y la noche,
el trabajo y la ira,
la sombra y la ternura,
todo lo has ido poco a poco cosiendo
a mis bolsillos rotos,
y no sólo en la zona trepidante
en que amor y martirio son gemelos
como dos campanas de incendio,
me esperaste, amor mío,
sino en las más pequeñas
obligaciones dulces.
El aceite dorado de Italia hizo tu nimbo,
santa de la cocina y la costura,
y tu coquetería pequeñuela,
que tanto se tardaba en el espejo,
con tus manos que tienen
pétalos que el jazmín envidiaría
lavó los utensilios y mi ropa,
desinfectó las llagas.
Amor mío, a mi vida
llegaste preparada
como amapola y como guerrillera:
de seda el esplendor que yo recorro
con el hambre y la sed
que sólo para ti traje a este mundo,
y detrás de la seda
la muchacha de hierro

V

A thread of wheat and water,
of crystal or of fire,
the word and the night,
work and anger,
darkness and tenderness,
all this you have been gradually sewing
into my torn pockets,
and you waited for me, my love,
not only in the quaking region
where love and martyrdom are twins
like two bells of fire,
but also in the smallest
of sweet domestic services.
The golden oil of Italy made your halo,
saint of the kitchen and the sewing-basket,
and your modest little trace of coquetry,
that kept you so long looking in the mirror.
With your hands that are tipped with
petals that the jasmine would envy
you washed up after meals, you washed my clothes,
and cleaned my bleeding wounds.
My love, into my life
you came prepared
like a poppy and like a partisan;
it is a silken splendour that I traverse
with the thirst and the hunger
which I brought into the world only for you,
and behind the silk
the iron maiden

que luchará a mi lado.
Amor, amor, aquí nos encontramos.
Seda y metal, acércate a mi boca.

who will fight by my side.
My love, my love, here we come together.
Silk and metal, come to my mouth.

VI

Y porque Amor combate
no sólo en su quemante agricultura,
sino en la boca de hombres y mujeres,
terminaré saliéndole al camino
a los que entre mi pecho y tu fragancia
quieran interponer su planta oscura.
De mí nada más malo
te dirán, amor mío,
de lo que yo te dije.
Yo viví en las praderas
antes de conocerte
y no esperé el amor sino que estuve
acechando y salté sobre la rosa.
Qué más pueden decirte?
No soy bueno ni malo sino un hombre,
y agregarán entonces el peligro
de mi vida, que conoces
y que con tu pasión has compartido.
Y bien, este peligro
es peligro de amor, de amor completo
hacia toda la vida,
hacia todas las vidas,
y si este amor nos trae
la muerte o las prisiones,
yo estoy seguro que tus grandes ojos,
como cuando los beso
se cerrarán entonces con orgullo,
con doble orgullo, amor,
con tu orgullo y el mío.

VI

And because Love joins battle
not only in its burning fields,
but also in the mouths of men and women,
I shall come out and face them on the road,
those who try to place their dark feet
between my breast and your fragrance.
There is nothing worse they can say
about me, my love,
than I have told you myself.
I lived on the prairies
before I knew you
and I did not wait for love to come,
I stalked it and threw myself on the rose.
What else can they tell you?
I am not good, not bad, just a man.
And then they will exaggerate the dangers
in my life, which you know
and which with your passion you have shared.
Ah well, that danger
is the danger of love, of absolute love
of all life,
of all lives,
and if this love should bring us
death or a prison cell,
I am certain that your wide eyes,
as when I kiss them,
then will close with pride,
with doubled pride, my love,
with your pride and mine.

Pero hacia mis orejas vendrán antes
a socavar la torre
del amor dulce y duro que nos liga,
y me dirán: – 'Aquella
que tú amas,
no es mujer para ti,
por qué la quieres? Creo
que podrías hallar una más bella,
más seria, más profunda,
más otra, tú me entiendes, mírala qué ligera,
y qué cabeza tiene,
y mírala cómo se viste
y etcétera y etcétera.'
Y yo en estas líneas digo:
así te quiero, amor,
amor, así te amo,
así como te vistes
y como se levanta
tu cabellera y como
tu boca se sonríe,
ligera como el agua
del manantial sobre las piedras puras,
así te quiero, amada.
Al pan yo no le pido que me enseñe
sino que no me falte
durante cada día de la vida.
Yo no sé nada de la luz, de dónde
viene ni dónde va,
yo sólo quiero que la luz alumbre,
yo no pido a la noche
explicaciones,
yo la espero y me envuelve,

But first they will pour words in my ears
to undermine the tower
of the sweet, harsh love that makes us one,
and they will tell me: 'That woman
whom you love,
she is not the woman for you,
why do you love her? I think
you could find someone more beautiful,
more serious, more profound,
more different, you know, see how flippant she is,
and look at that head of hers,
and what does she look like,
etcetera etcetera.'
And I say here in these lines:
that is how I want you, my love,
my love, that is how I love you,
just as you look now
and the way your mane
rises up and the way
your mouth smiles,
as lightly as water flows
from the spring over the clean stones,
that is how I like you, beloved.
I do not ask of bread that it should teach me
but that it be always there
every single day of my life.
I know nothing of the light, where it comes from
nor where it goes to,
I only want the light to illuminate.
I do not require of the night
explanations,
I wait for it to come and it wraps me round,

y así tú, pan y luz
y sombra eres.
Has venido a mi vida
con lo que tú traías,
hecha
de luz y pan y sombra te esperaba,
y así te necesito,
así te amo,
y a cuantos quieran escuchar mañana
lo que no les diré, que aquí lo lean,
y retrocedan hoy porque es temprano
para estos argumentos.
Mañana sólo les daremos
una hoja del árbol de nuestro amor, una hoja
que caerá sobre la tierra
como si la hubieran hecho nuestros labios,
como un beso que cae
desde nuestras alturas invencibles
para mostrar el fuego y la ternura
de un amor verdadero.

and so it is with you, you are
bread and light and darkness.
You came into my life
with everything you have about you,
formed
of light and bread and darkness as I expected you,
and that is how I need you,
that is how I love you,
and all those who want to hear tomorrow
what I shall not tell them, will have to read it here,
and stand back today because it is too early
for these arguments.
Tomorrow we shall give them only
a leaf of the tree of our love, one leaf
which will fall to earth
as if we had made it with our lips,
like a kiss falling down
from our insuperable heights
to show the fire and the tenderness
of a true love.

Epithalamium

Epitalamio

Epitalamio

Recuerdas cuando
en invierno
llegamos a la isla?
El mar hacia nosotros levantaba
una copa de frío.
En las paredes las enredaderas
susurraban dejando
caer hojas oscuras
a nuestro paso.
Tú eras también una pequeña hoja
que temblaba en mi pecho.
El viento de la vida allí te puso.
En un principio no te vi: no supe
que ibas andando conmigo,
hasta que tus raíces
horadaron mi pecho,
se unieron a los hilos de mi sangre,
hablaron por mi boca,
florecieron conmigo.
Así fue tu presencia inadvertida,
hoja o rama invisible
y se pobló de pronto
mi corazón de frutos y sonidos.
Habitaste la casa
que te esperaba oscura
y encendiste las lámparas entonces.
Recuerdas, amor mío,
nuestros primeros pasos en la isla:
las piedras grises nos reconocieron,

Epithalamium

Do you remember when
in winter
we came to the island?
The sea lifted up to us
a goblet of cold.
On the walls the creepers
rustled, letting fall
dark leaves
at our feet.
You too were a tiny leaf
that trembled on my breast.
The wind of life had blown you there.
At first I did not see you; I did not know
that you had been at my side
until your roots
pierced through my breast,
joined up with the trickles of my blood,
spoke through my mouth,
and flowered with me.
So your presence was unnoticed,
an invisible leaf or twig,
and suddenly my heart
was filled with fruits and sounds.
You lived in the house
that was waiting for you in darkness
and then you lit the lamps.
Remember, my love,
our first walks on the island:
the grey stones recognised us,

las rachas de la lluvia,
los gritos del viento en la sombra.
Pero fue el fuego
nuestro único amigo,
junto a él apretamos
el dulce amor de invierno
a cuatro brazos.
El fuego vio crecer nuestro beso desnudo
hasta tocar estrellas escondidas,
y vio nacer y morir el dolor
como una espada rota
contra el amor invencible.
Recuerdas,
oh dormida en mi sombra,
cómo de ti crecía
el sueño,
de tu pecho desnudo
abierto con sus cúpulas gemelas
hacia el mar, hacia el viento de la isla
y cómo yo en tu sueño navegaba
libre, en el mar y en el viento
atado y sumergido sin embargo
al volumen azul de tu dulzura.
Oh dulce, dulce mía,
cambió la primavera
los muros de la isla.
Apareció una flor como una gota
de sangre anaranjada,
y luego descargaron los colores
todo su peso puro.
El mar reconquistó su transparencia,
la noche en el cielo

and the gusts of rain,
the cries of the wind in the darkness.
But the fire
was our only friend,
next to the fire we embraced
sweet winter love
with all four arms.
The fire saw the growth of our naked kiss
until it touched hidden stars,
and it saw the birth and death of grief
like a broken sword
against the invincibility of love.
Remember,
you who sleep in my shadow,
how out of you grew
the dream,
from your naked breast
with its twin cupolas, open
to the sea, to the wind of the island
and how in your dream I sailed
free, on the sea and in the wind,
yet tethered and submerged
by the blue wealth of your sweetness.
Oh my sweet, my sweet,
spring transformed
the walls on the island.
A flower appeared like a drop
of orange-coloured blood,
and then the colours discharged
all their pure weight.
The sea reconquered its transparency,
night in the heavens

destacó sus racimos
y ya todas las cosas susurraron
nuestro nombre de amor, piedra por piedra
dijeron nuestro nombre y nuestro beso.
La isla de piedra y musgo
resonó en el secreto de sus grutas
como en tu boca el canto,
y la flor que nacía
entre los intersticios de la piedra
con su secreta sílaba
dijo al pasar tu nombre
de planta abrasadora,
y la escarpada roca levantada
como el muro del mundo
reconoció mi canto, bienamada,
y todas las cosas dijeron
tu amor, mi amor, amada,
porque la tierra, el tiempo, el mar, la isla,
la vida, la marea,
el germen que entreabre
sus labios en la tierra,
la flor devoradora,
el movimiento de la primavera,
todo nos reconoce.
Nuestro amor ha nacido
fuera de las paredes,
en el viento,
en la noche,
en la tierra,
y por eso la arcilla y la corola,
el barro y las raíces
saben cómo te llamas,

showed off its cloudy bunches
and now everything was whispering
our love-name, stone on stone
spoke our name and our kiss.
The island of stone and moss
resounded in its secret grottoes
like song in your throat,
and the flower that was born
in the cracks between the stones
with its secret syllable
spoke in passing your name,
the name of a burning plant,
and the craggy rock rising up
like the wall of the world
recognised my song, my beloved,
and everything spoke
your love, my love, beloved,
because the earth, time, the sea, the island,
life, the tides,
the seed in the earth
beginning to open its lips,
the devouring blossom,
the movement of spring,
all recognise us.
Our love was born
outside of walls,
in the wind,
in the night,
in the earth,
and because of this the clay and the blossom,
the mud and the roots
know your name,

y saben que mi boca
se juntó con la tuya
porque en la tierra nos sembraron juntos
sin que sólo nosotros lo supiéramos
y que crecemos juntos
y florecemos juntos
y por eso
cuando pasamos,
tu nombre está en los pétalos
de la rosa que crece en la piedra,
mi nombre está en las grutas.
Ellos todo lo saben,
no tenemos secretos,
hemos crecido juntos
pero no lo sabíamos.
El mar conoce nuestro amor, las piedras
de la altura rocosa
saben que nuestros besos florecieron
con pureza infinita,
cómo en sus intersticios una boca
escarlata amanece:
así conocen nuestro amor y el beso
que reúnen tu boca y la mía
en una flor eterna.
Amor mío,
la primavera dulce,
flor y mar, nos rodean.
No la cambiamos
por nuestro invierno,
cuando el viento
comenzó a descifrar tu nombre
que hoy en todas las horas repite,

and know that my mouth
joined itself to yours
because in the earth they sowed us together
and we were alone in not knowing it
and because we grow together
and flower together
and because of this
when we pass by
your name is on the petals
of the rose which grows in the stone,
my name is in the grottoes.
They know it all,
we have no secrets,
we grew together
but we did not know it.
The sea knows our love, the stones
of the rocky height
know that our kisses flowered
with infinite purity,
as from the gaps between them
a scarlet mouth appears;
so they know our love and the kiss
which join your mouth to mine
in an eternal flower.
My love,
sweet spring,
blossoms and sea surround us.
Let us not exchange that
for our winter,
when the wind
began to make out your name
which now it repeats all through the day,

cuando
las hojas no sabían
que tú eras una hoja,
cuando
las raíces
no sabían que tú me buscabas
en mi pecho.
Amor, amor,
la primavera
nos ofrece el cielo,
pero la tierra oscura
es nuestro nombre,
nuestro amor pertenece
a todo el tiempo y la tierra.
Amándonos, mi brazo
bajo tu cuello de arena
esperaremos
como cambia la tierra y el tiempo
en la isla,
como caen las hojas
de las enredaderas taciturnas,
como se va el otoño
por la ventana rota.
Pero nosotros
vamos a esperar
a nuestro amigo,
a nuestro amigo de ojos rojos,
el fuego,
cuando de nuevo el viento
sacuda las fronteras de la isla
y desconozca el nombre
de todos,

when
the leaves did not know
that you were a leaf,
when
the roots
did not know that you were searching for me
in my breast.
My love, my love,
spring
offers us heaven,
but the dark earth
is our name,
our love belongs
to all time and to the earth.
Loving each other, with my arm
under your sandy neck
we shall wait to see
how the earth changes, and time
on the island,
how the leaves fall
from the silent creepers,
how autumn flies off
through the broken window.
But we,
we shall wait
for our friend,
for our friend with red eyes,
the fire,
when the wind again
shakes the coasts of the island
and no longer knows the name
of all things,

el invierno
nos buscará, amor mío,
siempre,
nos buscará, porque lo conocemos,
porque no lo tememos,
porque tenemos
con nosotros
el fuego
para siempre.
Tenemos
la tierra con nosotros
para siempre,
la primavera con nosotros
para siempre,
y cuando se desprenda
de las enredaderas
una hoja
tú sabes, amor mío,
qué nombre viene escrito
en esa hoja,
un nombre que es el tuyo y es el mío,
nuestro nombre de amor, un solo
ser, la flecha
que atravesó el invierno,
el amor invencible,
el fuego de los días,
una hoja
que me cayó en el pecho,
una hoja del árbol
de la vida
que hizo nido y cantó,
que echó raíces,

then winter
will seek us out, my love,
always,
will seek us out, because we know it,
because we do not fear it,
because we have
with us
the fire
for ever.
We have
the earth with us
for ever,
spring with us
for ever,
and when a leaf
falls off
from the creepers
you know, my love,
what name will be written
on that leaf,
a name which is yours and mine,
our name of love, one single
being, the arrow
which flew through winter,
invincible love,
the fire of the days,
a leaf
which fell on my breast,
a leaf from the tree
of life,
which made its nest and sang,
which put down roots,

que dio flores y frutos.
Y así ves, amor mío,
cómo marcho
por la isla,
por el mundo,
seguro en medio de la primavera,
loco de luz en el frío,
andando tranquilo en el fuego,
levantando tu peso
de pétalo en mis brazos,
como si nunca hubiera caminado
sino contigo, alma mía,
como si no supiera caminar
sino contigo,
como si no supiera cantar
sino cuando tú cantas.

which gave flowers and fruits.
And so you see, my love,
how I walk
about the island,
about the world,
safe in the middle of spring,
crazed by light in the frost,
walking quietly through fire,
lifting your flower-petal
weight in my arms,
as if I had never travelled
except with you, my sweetheart,
as if I would not know how to travel
except with you,
as if I would not know how to sing
except when you sing.

Letter on my Travels

La carta en el camino

La carta en el camino

Adiós, pero conmigo
serás, irás adentro
de una gota de sangre que circule en mis venas
o fuera, beso que me abrasa el rostro
o cinturón de fuego en mi cintura.
Dulce mía, recibe
el gran amor que salió de mi vida
y que en ti no encontraba territorio
como el explorador perdido
en las islas del pan y de la miel.
Yo te encontré después
de la tormenta,
la lluvia lavó el aire
y en el agua
tus dulces pies brillaron como peces.

Adorada, me voy a mis combates.

Arañaré la tierra para hacerte una cueva
y allí tu Capitán
te esperará con flores en el lecho.
No pienses más, mi dulce,
en el tormento
que pasó entre nosotros
como un rayo de fósforo
dejándonos tal vez su quemadura.
La paz llegó también porque regreso
a luchar a mi tierra,
y como tengo el corazón completo

Letter on my Travels

Farewell, but you will be
with me, you will go with me
inside a drop of blood that flows in my veins
or outside, a kiss that scorches my face
or a belt of fire about my waist.
My sweet, accept
the great love that came out of my life
and which in you did not find a homeland
like the explorer, lost
in the islands of bread and honey.
I met you only
after the storm,
the rain cleaned the air
and in the water
your lovely feet gleamed like fish.

My adored one, I go to fight my battles.

I will scrape away the earth to make you a cave
and there your Captain
will wait for you with flowers in the bed.
Think no longer, my sweet,
of the anguish
that passed between us
like a ray of phosphorus
perhaps leaving us burned by its fire.
Peace came also because I am going back
to the struggle in my country,
and because my heart is filled

con la parte de sangre que me diste
para siempre,
y como
llevo
las manos llenas de tu ser desnudo,
mírame,
mírame,
mírame por el mar, que voy radiante,
mírame por la noche que navego,
y mar y noche son los ojos tuyos.
No he salido de ti cuando me alejo.
Ahora voy a contarte:
mi tierra será tuya,
yo voy a conquistarla,
no sólo para dártela,
sino que para todos,
para todo mi pueblo.
Saldrá el ladrón de su torre algún día.
Y el invasor será expulsado.
Todos los frutos de la vida
crecerán en mis manos
acostumbrados antes a la pólvora.
Y sabré acariciar las nuevas flores
porque tú me enseñaste la ternura.
Dulce mía, adorada,
vendrás conmigo a luchar cuerpo a cuerpo
porque en mi corazón viven tus besos
como banderas rojas,
y si caigo, no sólo
me cubrirá la tierra
sino este gran amor que me trajiste
y que vivió circulando en mi sangre.

with the share of blood that you gave me
for ever,
and because
my hands
are still full of your naked being,
look at me,
look at me,
look at me on the sea, which I travel radiantly,
look at me in the night through which I sail,
and sea and night are your eyes.
I have not left you when I travel afar.
Now I will tell you:
my country will be yours,
I am going to conquer it,
not only to give it to you,
but rather for everyone,
for all my people.
The robber will one day leave his tower.
And the invader will be driven out.
All the fruits of this life
will grow in my hands
until now accustomed only to gunpowder.
And I shall be able to caress the new flowers
because you taught me tenderness.
My sweet adored one,
you will come with me to fight hand to hand
because your kisses still live in my heart
like red banners,
and if I fall, not only
the earth will cover me
but also that great love that you brought me
and which lived circulating in my blood.

Vendrás conmigo,
en esa hora te espero,
en esa hora y en todas las horas,
en todas las horas te espero.
Y cuando venga la tristeza que odio
a golpear a tu puerta,
dile que yo te espero
y cuando la soledad quiera que cambies
la sortija en que está mi nombre escrito,
dile a la soledad que hable conmigo,
que yo debí marcharme
porque soy un soldado,
y que allí donde estoy,
bajo la lluvia o bajo
el fuego,
amor mío, te espero,
te espero en el desierto más duro
y junto al limonero florecido:
en todas partes donde esté la vida,
donde la primavera está naciendo,
amor mío, te espero.
Cuando te digan 'Ese hombre
no te quiere', recuerda
que mis pies están solos en esa noche, y buscan
los dulces y pequeños pies que adoro.
Amor, cuando te digan
que te olvidé, y aun cuando
sea yo quien lo dice,
cuando yo te lo diga,
no me creas,
quién y cómo podrían
cortarte de mi pecho

You will come with me,
in that hour I wait for you,
in that hour and in every hour,
in every hour I wait for you.
And when the sadness that I hate
comes knocking at your door,
tell it that I am waiting for you
and when loneliness wants you to change
the ring in which my name is written,
then tell loneliness to talk to me,
tell it that I had to march
because I am a soldier,
and that there where I am,
under rain or
under fire,
my love, I am waiting for you,
I wait for you in the harshest desert
and by the flowering lemon tree;
in every land where life exists,
where spring is born,
my love, I wait for you.
If they say to you 'That man
does not love you', remember
that my feet are alone in this night, and they
search for the sweet, tiny feet I adore.
My love, if they tell you
that I have forgotten you, and even if
it is I who say so,
if I should tell you this,
do not believe me.
By whom and how could you
be cut out from my breast,

y quién recibiría
mi sangre
cuando hacia ti me fuera desangrando?
Pero tampoco puedo
olvidar a mi pueblo.
Voy a luchar en cada calle,
detrás de cada piedra.
Tu amor también me ayuda:
es una flor cerrada
que cada vez me llena con su aroma
y que se abre de pronto
dentro de mí como una gran estrella.

Amor mío, es de noche.

El agua negra, el mundo
dormido, me rodean.
Vendrá luego la aurora,
y yo mientras tanto te escribo
para decirte: 'Te amo'.
Para decirte 'Te amo', cuida,
limpia, levanta,
defiende
nuestro amor, alma mía.
Yo te lo dejo como si dejara
un puñado de tierra con semillas.
De nuestro amor nacerán vidas.
En nuestro amor beberán agua.
Tal vez llegará un día
en que un hombre
y una mujer, iguales
a nosotros,

and who would collect
my blood
if it should flow out of me towards you?
But neither can I
forget my people.
I am going to fight in every street,
behind every stone.
Your love too will succour me;
it is a closed flower
which every time fills me with its perfume
and which suddenly opens
inside me like a great star.

My love, it is night.

The black waters, the world
in sleep, close me in.
Later dawn will come,
and in the meantime I write to you
to tell you: 'I love you'.
To tell you: 'I love you'; protect,
purify, lift up,
defend
our love, sweetheart.
I leave it to you as if I were leaving
a handful of earth full of seeds.
From our love lives will be born.
In our love they will drink water.
Perhaps a day will come
in which a man
and a woman,
just like us,

tocarán este amor, y aún tendrá fuerza
para quemar las manos que lo toquen.
Quiénes fuimos? Qué importa?
Tocarán este fuego
y el fuego, dulce mía, dirá tu simple nombre
y el mío, el nombre
que tú sola supiste porque tú sola
sobre la tierra sabes
quién soy, y porque nadie me conoció como una,
como una sola de tus manos,
porque nadie
supo cómo, ni cuándo
mi corazón estuvo ardiendo:
tan sólo
tus grandes ojos pardos lo supieron,
tu ancha boca,
tu piel, tus pechos,
tu vientre, tus entrañas
y el alma tuya que yo desperté
para que se quedara
cantando hasta el fin de la vida.

Amor, te espero.

Adiós, amor, te espero.

Amor, amor, te espero.

Y así esta carta se termina
sin ninguna tristeza:
están firmes mis pies sobre la tierra,
mi mano escribe esta carta en el camino,

will touch this love and it will still have the strength
to burn the hands of those that touch it.
Who were we? What does it matter?
They will touch this fire
and the fire, my sweet, will speak your simple name
and mine, the name
that you alone knew because you alone
on earth know
who I am, and because no one knew me like one,
like a single one of your hands,
because no one
knew how or when
my heart caught fire;
only
your great brown eyes knew it,
your wide mouth,
your skin, your breasts,
your belly, your entrails
and your soul which I awoke
so that it should keep on
singing until the end of life.

My love, I am waiting for you.

Farewell, my love, I am waiting for you.

My love, my love, I am waiting for you.

And so this letter ends
without any sadness;
my feet are firm on the ground,
my hand writes this letter on my travels

y en medio de la vida estaré
siempre
junto al amigo, frente al enemigo,
con tu nombre en la boca
y un beso que jamás
se apartó de la tuya.

and in the middle of life I shall be
always
next to my friend, facing the enemy,
with your name on my lips
and a kiss that never
went away from yours.

Spanish poetry from Anvil

Josep Carner
NABÍ
Translated from Catalan by J L Gili
Introduced by Arthur Terry
Bilingual edition

Luis de Góngora
SELECTED SHORTER POEMS
Translated by Michael Smith
Bilingual edition

Federico García Lorca
A SEASON IN GRANADA
Poetry and prose, compiled, translated
and introduced by Christopher Maurer

Federico García Lorca
LORCA: SELECTED POEMS
Introduced and edited by J L Gili

Justo Jorge Padrón
MEMORY OF THE FIRE
Selected poems 1989–2000
translated and introduced by Louis Bourne

For details of our range of classic and modern
poetry in translation, visit our website:
www.anvilpresspoetry.com